The Living Art of Chi Kung

Lizzie Slowe

Illustrations by Richard Verlander
forward by Nicola Ley

BALBOA.PRESS

A DIVISION OF HAY HOUSE

Balboa Press books may be ordered through booksellers or by contacting:

Balboa Press
A Division of Hay House
1663 Liberty Drive
Bloomington, IN 47403
www.balboapress.co.uk
UK TFN: 0800 0148647 (Toll Free inside the UK)
UK Local: (02) 0369 56325 (+44 20 3695 6325 from outside the UK)

All images and illustrations are by Richard Verlander.

Print information available on the last page.

ISBN: 978-1-9822-8474-9 (sc)
ISBN: 978-1-9822-8475-6 (e)

Balboa Press rev. date: 11/27/2021

Contents

Chi Kung

Moving Chi Kung forms

Living

Foreword

By Nicola Ley

I first met Lizzie Slowe before our children were even twinkles in their father's eyes. We were at a women's shiatsu retreat. We had all had a lovely time exploring energy and shiatsu in a group of like-minded women and laughing together. Laughter was one of Lizzie's greatest gifts. She had a way of being fully present in the energy field yet with a beautiful light touch.

After the retreat, while we were waiting to go home, Lizzie and I found ourselves in the beautiful garden. She taught me the Chi Kung form her shiatsu teacher, Chris Jarmey, taught at their Shiatsu school. I was entranced. Lizzie showed me the moves, which were fairly simple. Yet after our retreat and in the sunshine in a beautiful garden we touched something Divine. I still use that form.

It is fitting that I should mention her teaching here. She taught me to bring the lightness of sunshine, the butterfly passing by and the smile in each other's eyes all into the practice so that our Chi Kung was fully in the infinite Now. She showed me how to wriggle our newly painted toenails in the grass and appreciate the Earth and land beneath our feet. I think she had also brought the nail varnish to the workshop, so as well as a new Chi Kung form I went home with gloriously blue toenails.

I hope this book brings you some of the joy that underpins Lizzie's teaching. The ideas she brings here are clearly her sharing her practice with you. What she shares is what she has learnt from her years practising. It shows that what she learnt is to let the movements and exercises guide her to find what she needs. She knows the exercises are just a vehicle to move the Chi. She knows the Kung is the constant polishing of the vehicle.

I recommend this book of Chi Kung as containing some well-tuned vehicles. If you are needing to relax and connect to your body then the bareback horse ride will take you there. If you need to feel freer the vehicle will be a plane or a phoenix. Let Lizzie help you find the right vehicle which can take you on a journey of a lifetime.

Thank you for such a timely book. As the people in the world start to emerge from the Covid-19 pandemic we are all going to have to attend to our vehicles. The virus has taken a toll on our mental health, on many of our bodies and certainly our hearts. Our mind, our body and our hearts will all need attention as we step out in to the new world. The wonderful thing about Chi Kung is it helps all three. Everyone can find something to help their mind, body and heart in this book.

Nicola

Nicola Ley (Pooley) Locked down in Bristol, UK - 2021

Introduction

I was fortunate enough to train in Shiatsu and Chi Kung early in my twenties, and the frame of understanding that they offer has been invaluable. After over 25 years, I recently decided to stop practising Shiatsu, either just for now or for ever, I'm not sure yet. Instead, I've become more motivated to pass on some of the tools that have helped me so much, and to facilitate real change through experience and empowerment. Chi Kung has the potential to positively impact your physical, mental, emotional, and spiritual health and help you to find more comfort and ease. You really don't need to be an expert.

I've written this on and off over a two-year period. The second year of writing has been a year of turbulence in the whole world, as the Covid19 virus has disrupted life in many ways. It seems to me that the pandemic has triggered reactions in all of us - many of fear, some of frustration, anger, sadness, or a feeling of overwhelm - but whatever our reactions, they've been strong. Alongside this, there has been an upwelling of kindness and compassion, a shared experience and understanding, and a space to rest and reflect. I've hugely enjoyed the process of writing this book, and my hope is that it will contribute, however gently, to a shift towards more balance and harmony for both individuals and the wider whole.

The title 'The Living Art of Chi Kung' encapsulates my intention of taking the ancient Taoist art and making it accessible and relatable, of pointing towards possibilities, rather than being a focused academic text. I've aimed to convey the subtleties of practise and their relevance today, and provide an accessible manual for anyone who's interested in Chi Kung, or even just some body focused awareness.

So, I've split it into three parts.

The first, 'The Art', is composed of short sections describing the nuances and different elements of how and why to practise, and the ingredients that might make your approach effective or enjoyable.

The second section 'Chi Kung', contains descriptions and instructions of energetic structures, postures, warm ups and practises – some seated, some standing and some moving.

In the third section, 'Living', I've discussed a few bigger life topics, included some quotes from the Tao Te Ching (Using the excellent translation by Stephen Mitchell), and described how some aspects of life could be understood through a Taoist perspective and supported or informed through your Chi Kung practice.

Throughout I've used examples from my own life experience, and analogies developed through years of teaching, practising and facilitating. These are there to bring some of the messages to life, and ground some of my meanings in reality.

A little context on who I am; sometimes when I talk about my life it sounds colourful, even to me. I've travelled in India, lived in a Tipi in Wales, spent two years on a sailing boat and crossed the Atlantic with my young daughters. My education was at a music school as a classical cellist, I partied through the rave scene, overcame addictions, attended silent meditation retreats and even ran a marathon. One constant was change, even when I stopped moving and put down roots. I now count myself very lucky to feel stable in my home environment with family and friends (both human and animal). The change though hasn't stopped, for the last 10 years the change and adventuring has been more internally focused. Over the years, alongside Shiatsu and Chi Kung I've trained in Sports and Baby Massage, Reiki, Equine Shiatsu, Counselling and Equine Facilitated Therapy. These have all informed and expanded my skills and experience.

I've thoroughly enjoyed the process of writing, collecting some of my understanding and teaching into one place, and seeing the images in my mind interpreted and brought to life by a wonderful illustrator. I'm excited by the thought of sharing what I've learnt so far.

So with an open heart and a hope that I'm spreading a little joy, I sincerely hope you enjoy my book.

With warm wishes

Lizzie

The Art

Chi Kung and me

I consider myself to be an experiential Chi Kung practitioner and teacher. By that, I mean that I'm most interested in the felt experience that you (or I) have and in what we notice, rather than what the texts on the subject, or other people say we should or shouldn't be feeling. I don't have a particularly impressive lineage – I haven't completed an extended apprenticeship in a remote setting with an awakened master, nor am I any kind of awakened master myself.

I first came across Chi Kung by a happy accident. Having just returned from travelling in India, I found myself enrolled on a foundation course in Shiatsu (without even knowing what it was). It turned out that the teacher of the course was really into Chi Kung, and so the three weekends were spent learning the eighteen stance Tai Chi-Chi Kung form. That was over twenty-five years ago and what I'm now teaching, practising and writing about is my experiential understanding of how breath, movement, posture and attention can dramatically change our way of being. I've had many teachers with many different approaches, and each one has been valuable to me. My Chi Kung practice is of course also a product of life experience, as well as the influences of many wonderful Chi Kung students and peers.

We live in a society of great contrast and yet simultaneously of existing in bubbles where we think everyone thinks much as we do. I'm aware that people are drawn to Chi Kung for all kinds of reasons and from all kinds of backgrounds: some wanting to keep fit and strong into middle or old age; some seeking health, relief from symptoms, peace, calmer emotions or a quieter mind; some may be interested in Taoist philosophy or enlightenment; and some simply curious.

In a teaching situation I'm pretty good at reading my audience and pitching accordingly, but connecting with you through a book is a different game. I hope that you find something of use, and trust you'll discard whatever misses the mark.

Whether you're seeking awakening or just a good night's sleep, Chi Kung has the ability to boost and regulate the underlying energy of mind, body and spirit, which can have far reaching effects. It is though, of course, not a magic cure all – it's just Chi Kung, a practise that can help, but not the one and only thing you'll need in order to find eternal health and a blissful state!

Many teachers agree that meditation and spiritual practise don't have to mean sitting still on a cushion. Finding focus, presence, connection and awareness is easier once we're removed from everyday life and distraction, on a course or retreat with a skilled teacher. Much trickier is to live in our society, complete with families and communities, isolation, and pressures of fitting in etc, and find some level of peace and harmony in that frame.

Attention and Intention whilst doing anything have the capacity to change our experience and our very reality, in fact mindfulness as a way to create positive change is now a pretty mainstream concept. Chi Kung has much in common with mindfulness, but the forms, breathing and focus mean it is embodied and made physical, and therefore its reach is magnified. You *can* practise Chi Kung simply as a moving practise while thinking about something else – I've done plenty of Chi Kung in front of the TV and it does still have an effect. However, by a long way, most of the benefit comes when we have the intention to be present with the experience and effects in real time.

Some of the simplest Chi Kung exercises can be the most powerful, and can have varied effects depending on the focus and depth of practise. Chi Kung doesn't have to always take place in a specific practise session, there are spare pockets of attention dotted through most of our days. It can be toyed with and dabbled with in moments of opportunity, for instance while making dinner, running a bath, or at a bus stop. Every moment practised is useful.

This is not a book of all the Chi Kung forms, or even many of them. I've selected some of the simple forms with enough variation to keep a practise alive for many years. I've also included some that can be done with very limited mobility and require no stamina, in the spirit of making Chi Kung available to all, even some that are simply awareness practises. My intention is to offer enough in the way of tools and tips that I've opened the door to limitless possibilities of practise that can be explored.

The concepts of Chi Kung, Taoism and Wu Wei

When the philosophy and practise of Taoism was translated to English and other languages there was more than a little interpretation needed. We just don't have equivalent words and concepts for Chi Kung or Yin and Yang. Kung means something like effort, exercise, or practise. Chi is usually translated as energy or life force. Chi Kung is also often written Qi Gong – it was originally of course not in English so spell it how you like!

Although 'life force' and energy are in the English language, Chi as a concept doesn't have a real equivalent in the West. Either you'll be comfortable with the word energy or you won't. For those interested in Quantum Physics, the idea of 'a field' might get you closer to understanding the meaning. If 'energy' doesn't mean much to you, it might be easier to just use the word Chi, and find its meaning by experience rather than with your brain. Just ask yourself questions such as: which part of me feels the most alive right now? Or, what time of day do I find it easiest to get things done? Your answers will tell you where in your body the Chi is flowing best; and what time of day your Chi is flowing most easily. Simply by asking yourself questions you'll get an idea as to where your Chi feels strong and flowing, and where it feels weak or stuck.

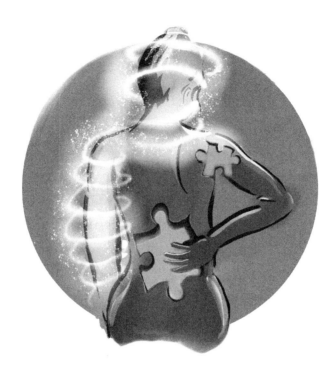

So, Chi Kung is a form of exercising your Chi. Chi (or your energy) affects and is affected by your physical, emotional, mental and spiritual ways of being, it has an impact across the spectrum of your experience. This is what makes its reach so vast.

Chi Kung is rooted in Toaist (pronounced dow (to rhyme with cow)-ist) philosophy. The Tao translates roughly as 'the way (of all things)'. The Tao Te Ching (the book of the way) is a book that was written, probably by a man named Lao Tzu, in time of Confucius. It describes Taoist philosophy and is the second most translated book in the world, an enduring source of timeless wisdom, discussing life, the universe, and everything. Much of it is as relevant today as it was in the 4th century BC when it was written.

Born out of a Taoist culture, I think Chi Kung must have originally come about by a spontaneous breath and movement, by someone one on a spiritual path seeking the Tao, or feeling their way towards greater well-being. It could've been a person's deliberate attempt to calm themselves, energise, heal or improve mobility. It must have been of benefit and been repeated and copied. Chi Kung was born out of a felt experience of moving Chi. At some point it became a 'thing', and this 'thing' in its many forms and lineages has been a part of Taoist culture since pre-historic China.

In Taoism there is a concept called Wu Wei which can be translated as effortless action, or action without intention. Born in a time where the rhythms of nature were much closer and more influential than they might be today, Taoism's concept of Wu Wei suggested that it was pointless to pit your effort or exert your will against the way of nature or the world, and if you did try, you would encounter unintended consequences. In Chi Kung this is absolutely encapsulated by the 'game' of making enough effort to practise, to be in a flowing posture, but also being relaxed and abdicating control of how your energy flows to avoid forcing the issue. It's about setting the scene, but not micromanaging the show. This gentle concept of 'as much as necessary and as little as possible', is most of the game of Chi Kung, and why for me, it never gets boring.

Yin and Yang

Taoist philosophy is most often represented by the notion of Yin and Yang, or opposites – any old opposites. Yang is the sunny side of the mountain, Yin the shaded side; Yang is warming, energetic, Yin is cooling, substantial; Yang is the moving, Yin the stillness etc. They are not fixed and always relative, so the sunny side of the mountain will have a highest part (Yang) and a lowest part (Yin). There is always Yin within Yang, and Yang within Yin.

Yin will always turn to Yang, and Yang will always turn to Yin, neither one is stable or constant, and one flows easily into the other. This is an important concept in Chi Kung as, although there is effort in the form and posture, any attempt or idea of trying to force something to happen or to keep something happening impedes the flow of Yin and Yang into each other. You might be deficient in Yin (a common pattern of disharmony according to Traditional Chinese Medicine), and want to do Chi Kung to cultivate more Yin. However, we also want to practise allowing and softening so that Yang can become Yin, the Yang is released into Yin, allowing universal balance to be restored. Uninhibited, Yin and Yang will always balance each other out, the problem is that we are both the inhibited and the inhibitors. These fluctuations occur through our internal and external environment; surroundings, work, relationships, thoughts and habits, feelings, posture and fitness and other influences. As long as flow is allowed, facilitated and encouraged if necessary, Yin and Yang will move through patterns of excess and deficiency and seek balance.

With practise and experience it's possible to sense the flow and 'what is' of Yin and Yang. In remembering that there is no absolute Yin or absolute Yang, perhaps we can start to wonder what the polar opposite of a sensation or a feeling might feel like. It's something that requires imagination and a felt understanding, which might (or might not) take time and practise.

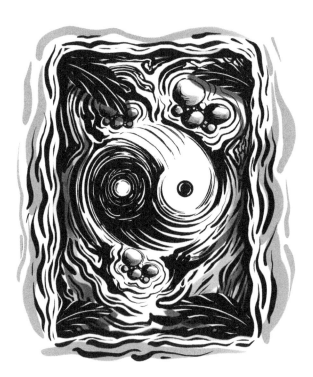

Meridians

Meridians are the map of the body followed by Acupuncturists, Shiatsu practitioners and some Traditional Chinese Medicine practitioners. They are typically referred to as 'energy channels' through which Chi circulates around the body, and looking at a meridian map conjures up an image of tubes or lines of energy – a little like the London Underground map. I find it more useful to think of them as currents in the whole-body flow, as opposed to channels, more like currents within an ocean. Ocean currents are powerful and flow between deep and shallow, as well as toward points of the compass, but they are not delineated as separate to the rest of the ocean, or even connected to the rest of the ocean. They *are* the ocean, and inseparable from the entirety.

The other thing I like to bear in mind is that maps don't always represent the landscape in real time. Just as the London Underground map is not a real map of London, the meridian map is not a real map of anyone's body. Using the analogy of water again, a current can be diverted by changes in the earth's climate, or the appearance of a new volcanic island or shifting tectonic plates. So can our Meridians be diverted by accident and injury, or chronic or genetic conditions. In general, if we look for them using the landmarks of the body, a little like a kind of geocaching or treasure hunt, with a bit of feeling around and a bit of practise we can find them, even if they have had to adapt around a changing body.

I do use meridians, and acupressure points (as well as other energetic structures of the body) in Chi Kung. My experience both as a Shiatsu practitioner and a Chi Kung teacher have shown me that they are both real and impactful. In this book you'll find descriptions of what I find are the most useful acupressure points in Chi Kung practise, as well as a couple of energetic structures of the body and a couple of meridians.

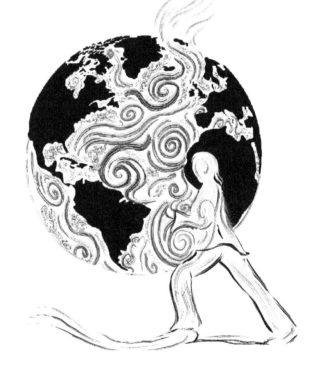

The Benefits of Chi Kung. Feeling better

There are many benefits to Chi Kung, and they're not limited to just physical. This is another place where our language and cultural understanding trips us up. Feeling better is something that has come to mean many things. You can have an awful lot wrong with you but take some smashing painkillers and 'feel better'... You can have a broken heart and stuff vast quantities of ice-cream and 'feel better'... you can think if only others would behave differently you would 'feel better'. But none of these is what I'm referring to.

The type of feeling better that Chi Kung can offer isn't dependent on anything external changing in the world. Chi Kung is a practise that works within your own body/mind, without changing anything outside yourself. Taking a painkiller can be a little like taking the battery out of a smoke alarm, eating a ton (or maybe just a tub) of ice-cream can numb your body to its feeling sensations, and wanting someone else to change to make you happier is an unrealistic (and slightly selfish) expectation.

As a society in general we are also great at diversion from discomfort, the dreaded screens do this well, but even going for a run or tidying up can easily be used as avoidance strategies. Chi Kung is taking an active interest in how you really are within the confines of yourself. It's a compassionate, sometimes brave, and attentive conversation between you and you – or your mind and the entirety of your being.

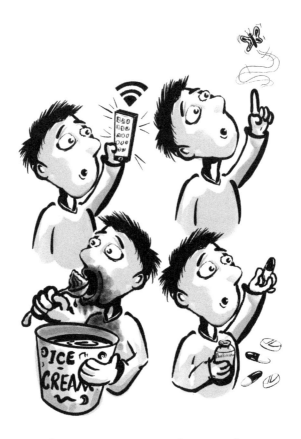

This might mean that you're starting from a place you've been avoiding if you've been using distraction or other strategies to feel better. It really doesn't matter, because if you're getting real with yourself it's a huge step towards feeling better already, in fact you can't start to feel better until you do. Wherever you're starting from you might be surprised just how easily symptoms, apathy or discomfort start to shift by practising Chi Kung. It has, simply by means of improving the flow of energy in your body, the capacity to improve feelings of physical, mental, emotional and even spiritual comfort and vitality. It is amazing what can change from doing a practise that seems so simple.

How it works

Chi Kung is simple, but not necessarily easy. It's based on an understanding of how wellbeing works, which was developed purely by observation, during a time in history when dissection was not permitted, so the inner workings of the body were not as important as noticing the external manifestations. Noticing what worked and what didn't, and observing the interaction of all parts of our being and environment was the foundation of the Taoist understanding of health.

Good health was viewed as something to cultivate and constantly work on, and doctors were only paid when patients stayed healthy. Good health was synonymous with contentment and spiritual advancement, and was an investment to be nurtured and built. It was noticed and understood that simply by practising breath and gentle movement in combination with awareness, a person's full health and resilience could be improved.

Chi follows awareness, and so wherever we take our focus our Chi will follow. The power of awareness and intention is increased and magnified by breath and movement, and by practise. Imagine that you're trying to 'waft' something along, like smoke. Imagine that you want this smoke to go a certain way, maybe into a corner. It may take a while until you get the hang of the best way to do it. If you carried on a bit hit and miss without paying attention to which kind of swooshing movement got the smoke to move the right way, you'd certainly get the smoke to move around, and you'd get some occasional successes but at least as much smoke would escape into the rest of the room. If you were really interested in what the most effective swooshing movement was, you'd probably get very effective over time and with practise.

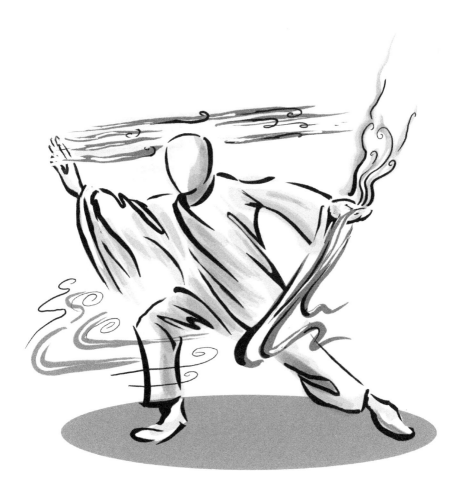

Chi Kung, 'energy exercises' are similar, in that we are swooshing Chi through our physical, mental, emotional and spiritual selves. Through practising with interest how Chi Kung feels, over and over we can cultivate a felt understanding of its effects.

By standing and moving from an aligned posture, we're creating a physical landscape where flow is most likely, or able, to happen. And by using movement, posture, mind and breath together, we can increase the flow and circulation of Chi through the body. We have the possibility to purposefully or accidentally influence our functioning. We can allow stagnant or excessive Chi (which can cause symptoms and unnecessary drains on our system) to resolve and relax. We can also increase the flow, quality and quantities of Chi, fortifying and supporting our system.

That is my best description of how Chi Kung works, but you will find your own felt sensation which will be most meaningful to you.

What we notice

When I first started to study Shiatsu and practise Chi Kung, my peers always seemed to be 'sensing the energy' or getting 'releases' or 'spontaneous movements of Chi'. I noticed nothing particularly, and secretly fluctuated between thinking they were making it up or that I was devoid of feeling. Over my years of practise, I've refined my senses to be able to really observe much more of what was already there in the first place. Part of the problem for me was that I was used to very crude and loud external stimuluses. Pounding rave music (don't judge me!), action films, shopping centres, strong tasting food and drinks, theme parks and advertisements all shout very loud. It makes listening to the subtle movements of our own energy harder. Listening to our own body still really only happens for most people either with pain or discomfort, which we can easily hide from in fear (of disease or other worries) or guilt (for instance over having eaten too much sugar or lack of exercise) or blame (our job makes us too sedentary or our days are just too busy). Unfortunately, this is a completely normal state of being for many of us, and realistically just a part of the human condition for us unenlightened mortals! When we stop hiding and face our discomfort it's often because our body has shouted at us so loudly, we can no longer ignore it. If we begin doing awareness exercises and Chi Kung in this state it will likely take a little while before we can 'hear' the movement of energy over the shouting of our body.

However, even from this state (and more easily with a slightly less urgent body) within a few sessions of practising Chi Kung or mind body awareness exercises many people are able to start to feel something – often some tingling, or aliveness, or even a slight improvement in vitality or comfort, even if at first this is only for short periods. It's a bit like we're tuning our radio station to white noise instead of focusing on a particular radio station, and listening to what is there all the time in the back ground. Like learning to pay attention to the screen that the film is being projected on to – to yourself and not all the things that happen to you.

Although I say that I didn't feel anything for a few years when I started down this road, that isn't strictly true. Something in what I was doing must have felt good or helpful to me – because I continued practising anyway.

A note on focus and outcome

"If you do what you've always done, you will get what you've always got". (quote attributed to Jessie Potter, Tony Robinson and more). I often describe Chi Kung and in particular the warmups as a conversation between you and your body, which involves listening as well as talking! Making the tiniest of adjustments as you listen can change the course of your practise. Becoming curious about where and how you experience sensations in your body, and noticing your patterns, such as pushing, holding, bracing or compensating is all that is required. Trying to make the exterior look like you are doing good Chi Kung at the expense of this interior exploration takes the Chi (or the energy) out of Chi Kung. By staying as present as you can in the experience, you'll increase the impact of your Chi Kung tenfold.

In 2020 did a 1:1 zoom session with a Chi Kung student who normally attends my class but hadn't for a while due to the Covid lockdown. She is someone who really listens to instruction, and is genuinely interested in improving her health and hearing what I have to say. She also has a regular practise at home – something that sounds easier to do than it really is! During the zoom session I became aware that although her shoulders were not raised and her chest looked open enough, there was no softness in her structure in that area. We worked together on breathing and softening from her throat downwards as we moved through a form together. The difference was marked, she felt a shift in sensation, and her comment was that it was nice to have some feedback and do some proper Chi Kung. By that, she meant that she had been doing all the right things but in the same way that she did everything. The part of her that was in effect cut off from the flow of Chi was the part that she didn't notice – because it was cut off!

In psychotherapy the idea that every person can only see life through their own lens of their own conditioning is well understood. It's not rose-tinted glasses, but (in my case) Lizzie tinted glasses, and we all have our own tint. Because of this we are often blind, numb, deaf etc to our own patterns of being. This makes going to a Chi Kung class or a teacher for feedback really useful. It also makes an attitude of courageous undefended curiosity the most valuable asset you can have.

Chi Follows Awareness

"Where your attention goes your Chi will follow" One of the most important parts of the moving and breathing meditation that is Chi Kung, is your attention. The biggest effect we can have on anything is how we attend to it. Observation changes outcome and this discovery of Quantum Physics holds true for Chi Kung. Depending on where you choose to look you will experience and actually create very different realities.

The quality of awareness can be hard to cultivate. When we 'try' to feel something we often get in the way with our trying. If I ask you to become aware of your breath as it is, many of you will have automatically tried to deepen your breath as opposed to observing it as it is. Our understanding of what we 'ought' to feel like or look like, often overrides the truth of how we are. So, an interested observation without weighting an experience or sensation as good or bad is invaluable.

In Chi kung of course we often want to influence, to improve, before we even check in with where we are. But we need to put our boat in the water where we actually are in order to flow downstream in the direction we desire. The quality of Wu Wei, or practise without expectations, helps us to flow without trying to paddle against the current.

One of the most effective practises which engages awareness is to simply notice, to make the unconscious conscious.

Awareness that is truly interested in discovering and learning has an open and expansive quality to it, a spacious feeling rather than a tight focusing feeling, an open observation rather than a searching or superimposing.

Employing your own awareness is the best teacher and learning tool, and will give power and purpose and the possibility of real improvement to your Chi Kung practise.

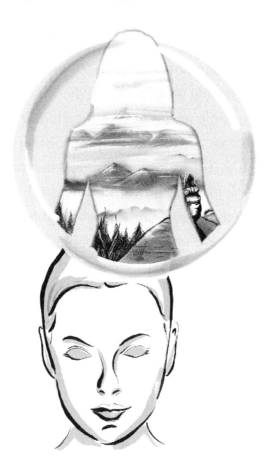

A note on trying and effort

The Yin and Yang of 'efforting' and allowing is at the centre of much of Chi Kung practise. And it really is Yin and Yang. Yes, Chi Kung requires effort, but trying hard will likely get in your way. It's a balancing act of effort and ease, trying and allowing, strength and softness.

In order for lightness to feel easy, and like it's flowing downstream, it needs to be held with security and gentle strength. If we don't have that sense of easy strength to fall back on, it will be harder to surrender our grip without fear of wobbling.

Without softness however, we can't make space for our Chi to flow and as we'll be blocking with tension. We simply can't force the Chi to flow by strength. We can allow it to flow, and we can use strength to hold space for it to flow in, but there must be an openness within which the Chi can move. Using as little tension as possible to move in a form creates a kind of frictionless flow capable of allowing Chi move through us. This can feel a bit like trying not to try!

This Yin and Yang of trying applies both to our mental state and our physical state.

Mentally we want to stay engaged and interested, and yet not so determined that we grit our teeth and scrunch our toes in effort. Letting go of striving and trying to understand and analyse can liberate vast amounts of Chi almost instantly. I love the analogy that letting go of effort and tension can feel like a cork being held under water and then released up to the surface where it can float easily.

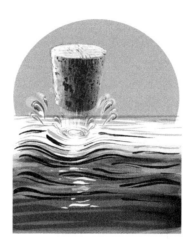

At the same time, Chi Kung requires concerted and continuous application. We're invited to move beyond exisisting in our familiar internal patterns of energy, some of which will be creating resistance. We start to notice how our minds can contract, or expand and we're asked to explore our internal state with our awareness and imagination. In order to recognise and release internal conflict, unearth denial and relinquish struggle, our self observation needs to be engaged and courageous.

On the physical plane, most Chi Kung in part requires us to build strength. Deep standing for instance (described in the Chi Kung section) builds strength where we need it, in our standing apparatus - the biggest muscles in our body. In our culture, our everyday life often exercises our screen using muscles, and our upper body as we move around less with our legs but do more reaching with our arms and working with our hands. Chi Kung often requires us to use easy strength in our lower body to support a light and flowing upper body.

It's also useful to distinguish strength from tension. Once the strength has been built, it's there if we need it. We have plenty of spare capacity that we don't necessarily need to use all the time, and it's from there that we can discover lightness.

(Yin within Yang and Yang within Yin don't forget – we also need lightness in the lower body and strength in the upper body!)

To find lightness in the upper body, here is an experiment you can play with. If you hold your arms up and out to the sides, and then just release completely, they should just flop messily down by your sides and then come to stillness. Once you have felt that, lift your arms again and try to let go a few muscle fibres at a time, letting go, and letting go, until you've let go so much that your arms flop down as before. You can then go back to holding up your arms and see if you can release as many of your muscle fibres as possible, until you get to just before your arms flop down. It might feel as if your arms are being suspended by magic. If you can get to this place, you're using as much as necessary and as little as possible, just where we want to position ourselves for Chi Kung.

We aim to use enough effort to sit or stand in a posture that accommodates spaciousness, build the strength to hold our shape easily without having to constantly try, and encourage softness to dissolve habitual conflict, allowing our chi to flow towards more harmony.

Putting in effort to that effect will be very productive!

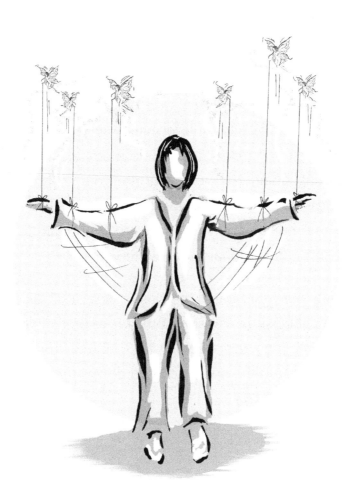

A note on limitations

You may be coming to Chi Kung from an already vibrant and healthy place. Or you may (like I did) be coming to Chi Kung to try to find health and well-being that you perhaps once took for granted but is now elusive or a distant memory. You may have never been comfortable or happy in your body, or you may just be seeking ease and a little more vitality. Wherever your starting point, I hope to nurture your enthusiasm and the limitless possibilities that await you, as it is all achievable. In the same breath, I would urge you to be realistic in your expectations, and compassionate with yourself.

The saying 'put your boat in the water where it is" (as opposed to dragging it up stream to start somewhere preferable), is very relevant here. You can start practising Chi Kung from wherever you are, just get in the boat and head downstream.

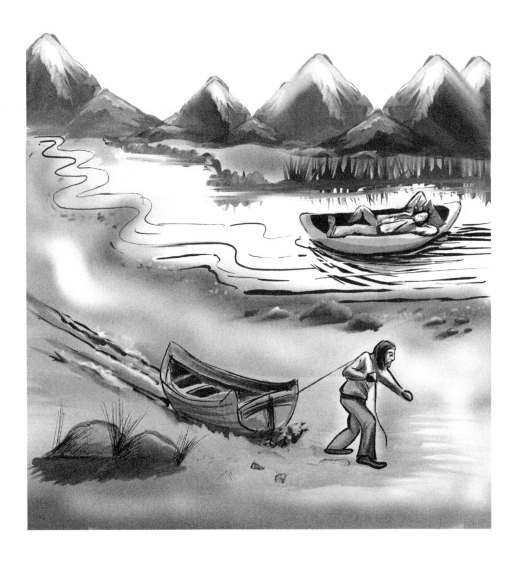

Many people use their symptoms or lack of health as reasons to beat themselves up, to berate themselves and impatience to improve can in itself be one of the biggest barriers to improvement.

The Tao Te Ching tells us "Not knowing is true knowledge. Presuming to know is a disease. First realize you are sick; then you can move toward health."

When I began practising Chi Kung, I had IBS following a year of travelling in India, one or two unhelpful addictions and a smattering of self-loathing and judgement, as well as a tendency to feel like a helpless victim of my circumstances. I'm not saying that all of this was resolved by learning Chi Kung alone, but it was a starting point that allowed me to do something positive for and with myself, and the beginning of a softening which allowed change (through many different avenues) to begin. The Taoist principles of simplicity, patience and compassion held me through and beyond that time, with a gentle and undemanding practise. Chi Kung was suited to exactly where I was at the time, and my practise has evolved with me.

There is a lovely description of how Chi Kung can help you to build health. Every time you do a practise, you put a sheet of paper on a pile. One practise = one sheet of paper. It doesn't matter whether you then practise the next day or two years later, the next practise puts another sheet of paper on top of the first, and as you continue you make a pile of paper. This pile of paper represents your 'stack of good health and wellbeing'. It doesn't shrink with neglect... any practise you do is health in the bank, and it can only be added to.

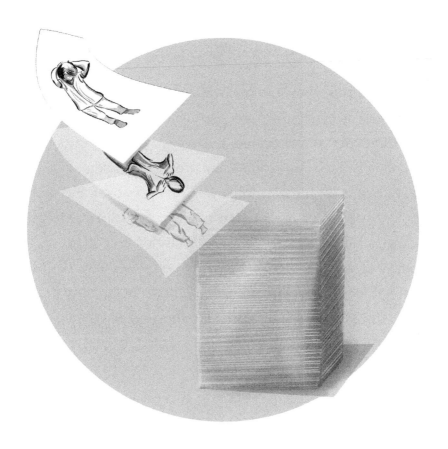

We are all starting from different places with our practise, and it is essential that you listen to your body before listening to me or anyone else. If you feel discomfort then pushing through is not always (or even often) the answer. Our culture has taught us that powering through is to be celebrated, and giving in is weak. We applaud demanding, arduous journeys that result in victory or success, and there are many sayings to the effect that 'nothing that comes easily is worth having'. I disagree that struggling against the tide is inevitable, but things do get tough sometimes, and sometimes the struggle is of our own making.

When navigating any journey, within yourself or through life, a search for ease, a steady pace, pausing, breathing and checking your direction are invaluable. It can help to look way into the distance to check your course, but progress is made by taking a step at a time. In the way that a stream flows over and around whatever obstacles it encounters, and eventually carves out a canyon, so a sense of patience and consideration of our starting point, will give us the long term benefits we may desire. In short – listen to your body. If you are not sure 'go easy side' as one of my teachers used to say. Find the edge of where you are able to relax and work just inside it.

A note on stretching

Stretching out tight muscles and connective tissue is always a good idea. If you do any kind of sports, or even a lot of walking, it's pretty safe to say that you probably need to stretch much more than you do. However, it's again important not only that we do stretch, but how to do it. There's a difference between practising exercises that work on the physical body (tissues, nerves, fascia etc) and practising Chi Kung, which works across the physical and energetic bodies as they are one. Forcing a stretch can cause a contraction of energy, and bouncing in a stretch has no lasting benefits. It is usual to see people grunting and holding their breath, and wincing as they stretch with resistance instead of relaxation. I like to use the image of allowing yourself to melt into the stretch (I always imagine melting chocolate but that's just me) and that can take a little time.

Relaxing in a stretch is of course much easier if you are realistic about how far you can stretch without gritting your teeth! Finding a place where you can really relax and feel a stretch at the same time is key, and I'd encourage you to play around with your anatomy in any stretch to find a good spot for yourself.

Breathing (especially the out breath) will help to counter contraction, and a deep breath in followed by a sigh will often help with letting go. It's worth mentioning that I often see people doing the very purposeful, noisy and slightly panicky breathing that accompanies effort and discomfort, which has nothing to do with letting go!

I do believe that stretching is important as part of a healthy life, and opening creases and corners that are often neglected is a wonderful way to promote the flow of Chi in your body. There are forms of Chi Kung that can give you a good stretch, but there is no reason that Chi Kung should be your only practise. A good Yoga teacher (I have found that Yin Yoga is especially compatible), or bodyworker (such as Shiatsu) can work well alongside your Chi Kung practise or even an intuitive 5 minutes of stretching out freestyle, if you are called to in-depth stretching as a form of building health.

A note on Breath

As mentioned above in reference to stretching, how you breathe can be a game changer. It can both affect how you're feeling, and be an indication that we're feeling something. We all have different breathing habits and capacities. Unconscious breath holding happens to all of us, and usually when breathing would be useful.

There are many advanced breathing practises associated with Taoism, but initially I am a fan of breathing in general, the easier and more enjoyable the better.

Instead of telling you the correct way to breathe, I'd like to bust a couple of assumptions about breathing.

Despite what you may have been told, it's not always better to breathe slower, especially not if it is making you feel panicky. There's an assumption that you should be able to take long slow breaths, but it's really about what works for you without comparison to anyone else. They're your lungs, so you set the pace.

Another breathing assumption many of us have, is that we're supposed to breathe into our belly. As I'm sure you know, your lungs are in your rib cage. So, anatomically, as you breathe in, your shoulders may rise, your rib cage will expand, and your diaphragm will push down towards your belly. There is no lung capacity in your belly, it just gets a little sort of squish when your diaphragm pushes down. As your diaphragm descends, your tummy will feel like it's pushing out a bit. So, with a realistic physical focus, breathe air into your lungs, and not your belly.

One practise that I like to teach is to just breathe into the part of your lungs that feels easiest. When you find the part of the lungs that's most enjoyable for you to breathe in and out of, practise breathing into that part. Eventually the sense of pleasure or enjoyment in the breath will spread and overflow into other parts of your lungs. If finding any joy in breathing is difficult for you, try imagining that the air is supercharged, clear, refreshing, even full of magic vitality. And it's absolutely free!

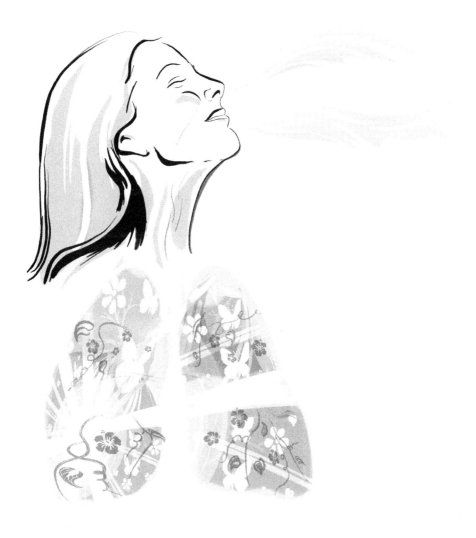

If you are able, breathing through your nose is preferable, especially on the in-breath. Sometimes, a deep sigh, breathing fully in through your nose and just letting the air rush out through your mouth feels good, and helps you to 'reset' and release tension. If you're purposefully breathing but sounding like Darth Vader you're possibly not finding the relaxation or vitality in the breath that you're seeking. Try allowing your face to be soft, throat open, and let the air enter and leave the lungs in a way that feels as easy and frictionless as possible.

Perhaps my favourite breathing practise is for the In and Out breath to be equal in length, and to pause for just a moment at the bottom of the outbreath and again at the top of the inbreath, to find just a moment of suspension between the breaths. It can feel like a moment of freedom or stillness.

When practising Chi Kung, it is absolutely appropriate to breathe, any breath is good, so keep it comfortable, and through your nose if possible, allowing the breath to enter and leave your body freely.

Breathing is often seen in meditation as the bridge between the mind and body. In Chi Kung it's a part of that bridge, as moving, breathing and awareness combine to unite your physical and energetic body. Moving through Chi Kung practises without breath just doesn't really work. If you find it hard to breathe in the prescribed places, just breathe. In fact, in general, in life, just breathe.

A note on being present

Our attention will often wander, especially if we're practising an exercise on our own, and not in a class with someone talking it through. This is completely normal; it's what minds do.

In fact, our attention is never static, trying to hold it in one place won't work for very long. Like a vibration, our minds or awareness constantly oscillate very fast between expansion and contraction. So fast that we couldn't possibly follow the oscillation with our very slow brains. We can imagine it depicted like a radio wave, with peaks and troughs.

When we're trying to tune into an expanded state of awareness (opening our peripheral vision and awareness to encompass more than we can consciously process) we're actually tuning into peak after peak after peak, and not holding one continuous state. Likewise, when we're focusing our awareness or mind (honing in on a detail or single point) we are tuning into trough after trough after trough. Trying to hold either state will meet with resistance eventually as yin and yang, or expansion and focus start to try to balance.

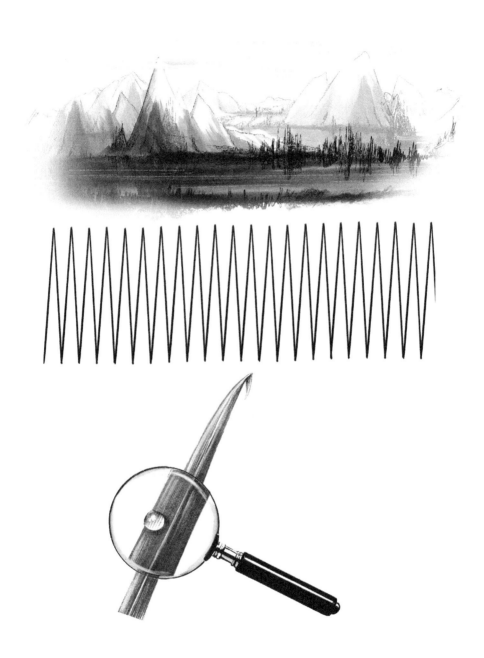

You can experience this for yourself quite easily. Focus on a point – it could be on the wall or on a page, anywhere, and start really trying to see as specific a thing as possible. As you try to maintain your focus, keeping it really specific and intense, at some point you will realise that the urge to zone out has overtaken you and your awareness has expanded.

In fact, as you expand your awareness for just a moment, you take in much more information than you can process. In that moment you have taken in everything, but not thought about anything. You can experiment with this by expanding your awareness and then, after the moment, remembering what you felt.

Here's a way of trying it. Take your awareness to your whole body – but do it just for a moment, expand your awareness out and then let it go. Don't start doing a tour, or searching for a feeling or sensation, just do it in a snapshot. Once it has been done and the moment has passed, you can reflect on what you felt, by remembering. It's as if you took a feeling photo, then get to peruse it at your leisure. Compare this to the experience of going searching through your body looking for sensations, where you might find it's easier to get lost in thoughts.

Our brains can be like pattern matching machines, we predict based on past experience and fill in many blanks all the time. If we want to truly be present with our experience, we can keep renewing our expansion (tuning in to the peaks) and know that there will be a time to reflect back on the experience,

By avoiding our predicative brain's assumptions, we can feel what's real right now, and in this way, we may notice a new detail, or something surprising and different.

I sometimes get headaches, and find myself wishing my whole head felt better. On investigation I'm usually able to find some comfortable areas of my head, or find that the pain originates somewhere unexpected. I've even ended up chasing pain around my head in a sort of cat and mouse game, as it seems to be avoiding attention.

Attention comes and goes, none of us are focused or expanded all the way through our practise. The most important thing to remember is that this is normal. Spacing out is unwanted expansion, and overthinking is our brains trying to focus in. Both will always be a part of your experience. By getting familiar with the process, you can at least have some understanding and compassion for yourself as you navigate your own vibration. Finding ourselves overthinking, and drifting off; wondering if we have practised long enough; it's just what we do. No big deal.

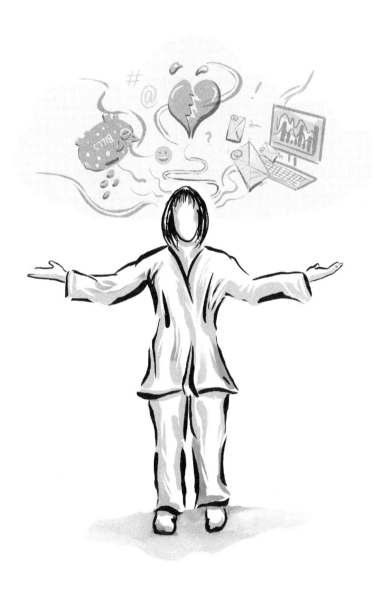

Having a regular practise

As with everything, having a regular Chi Kung practise has Yin and Yang, or opposing themes and qualities to it, such as discipline and spontaneity, or commitment and freedom.

For many of us a disciplined practise can be elusive. Making unrealistic goals and then failing to achieve them will leave us feeling worse than if we hadn't made a goal in the first place. However, that doesn't mean we should just give up! An ad hoc practise is vastly better than no practise at all, and there is much to be said for a less prescriptive approach. You may find that waiting to be moved to practise leads you to practising at random times and with authentic spontaneity, which is likely far more productive than forcing a practise into a 10-minute slot between doing the washing up and leaving for work just because you promised yourself that you would.

Certainly, there are many traditions where a regimented and dedicated practise is seen as the only path, for instance in the world of sports and athletics as well as in some meditative and yogic practises. Time spent in training or practise is seen as directly relational to understanding and achievement.

In truth, almost everyone has one or two ten-minute pockets spare each day, or at least three times a week, and most of us could squeeze half an hour of something in if we really wanted to prioritise it. However, being able to commit to and sustain a regular practise can be a hard thing to do, and often seem just out of reach.

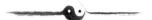

Over many years I played the game of self-berating, thinking that if only I could stick to a daily practise (or giving up sugar; or meditating for 20 minutes a day or...) my health (mental, emotional or physical) would be better. But just like all ingredients for good health, it doesn't always have to be all or nothing. The Taoist principles of simplicity, patience and compassion can guide us through, negating the need for self-flagellation at missing a session or even not starting to begin with. Remind yourself that every moment practised is an investment in your health. So even if you are an occasional practitioner, or you've missed a session or a week, you can continue without any loss.

A regular practise can look different for everyone. For some it might be every Sunday, or once a week in a class. For others it might be simply five minutes every evening, or an hour three times a week. You get the idea, there are as many ways to practise as you can think of. The most important thing is that it should fit into your life – and we all have our own shape for this. Having said that, a regular practise of some kind is extremely beneficial, as the more you practise, the more you will experience as you become more familiar with what you're working with (yourself and your Chi). My experience, sensation and understanding has significantly deepened when I have practised more – seems obvious really.

Much of how you approach your Chi Kung depends on your motivation for practising, often a combination in varying ratios of carrot and stick.

If you are having a large scary health crisis, and life is giving you a loud warning to take some action, you may have been given the motivation to prioritise a substantial practise. If this is the case and you feel able to commit, you will absolutely see results if you do Chi Kung every day for around an hour, and even up to an hour and a half. I've known more than one person who had big crises such as Cancer and AIDS, and with dedicated Chi Kung practise (often many hours each day) found their way back to good and vibrant health. However, without such loud and scary motivation, such a practise can be hard to find.

What is more important than having a frequent or regular practise by a long way, is how you approach each session. Turning up in Wu Chi, when you would much rather, or feel that you ought to be doing something else, is unlikely to progress your experience. Knowing in your head that Chi Kung is something you're doing to improve your health and well-being when your heart is telling you to have a bath or get on with making food, has already set up conflict in your body. I'm not expecting anyone to suddenly find that time just offers itself up for your practise. More that we notice our inner conflicts around doing some Chi Kung for and with ourselves, notice them and allow them. Being able to be flexible instead of rigid, compassionate instead of regimented, and patient as opposed to impatient, will more likely encourage our heart to join with our head's intention to practise Chi Kung.

If having any kind of practise is a challenge for you, be kind to yourself. Below are some tips that have worked for me at different times when I've been struggling, which may be useful to you if need help to get going.

Make your practise the easy side of manageable, shorter rather than longer. Leave yourself wanting more!

It doesn't have to be daily, it's fine to work around your commitments – for example two or three practises a week.

Re-frame: for instance, replace 'I *must* practise Chi Kung' with something like 'I'm just going to play with a little Chi Kung'.

Commit to short stretches at a time. For example, focus on a week or a couple of days to start with, and only focus on another couple of days / week if you've completed and enjoyed the first.

Don't be tempted to up the pressure on yourself by increasing week on week so it becomes less fun or unmanageable. You can always make your practise shorter instead of longer.

Get a bit creative with it, for instance make your only goal to stand in Wu Chi four times a day.

If it's helpful, make your daily practise at the same time each day. Be wary however that you don't drag yourself through a daily practise in desperation, but follow the art of practising with simplicity, patience and compassion.

One you have turned up to your practise session, set an alarm so that you're not tempted to clock watch. This way you can indulge in your inner exploration uninterrupted.

The struggle is often to just turn up, to just start each practise. I find that once I've turned up and have planted my feet on the ground, I feel relieved to have found the space, and practicing Chi Kung then becomes a pleasure.

Making any real change, although seemingly simple, is very hard to do. Even the smallest change can have ripples that touch every corner of our lives, so there is every reason to persist.

Allowing myself to practise freely, without feeling that I ought to do more or more often is something that I still find slippery to this day. I'm even writing a book about Chi Kung and I don't have a regimented practise! However, I remind myself that every time I practise Chi Kung it's a sheet of paper in my health bank, every practise is helpful.

How to approach a persistent sensation

Some people practising Chi Kung will at some point become aware of a sensation, (often experienced as a feeling, thought or image as described by Dan Siegel, author of Mindsight) which is persistent. A sensation that's enjoyable isn't a problem, and usually shows we're on the right path. The body's a good barometer like that. An unpleasant sensation can be a cause of irritation, frustration, or even anxiety, and can leave us feeling like we must be doing something wrong and wanting to fix it immediately.

It can be all too easy for a sensation to trigger a train of thought. And a train of thought is just that. Trains can only run on tracks in one direction, and so once a thought train has been triggered, it will always run the same way away from the sensation.

A sensation is often our body trying to communicate with us. In order to get a different result from a sensation, we can approach it in a different way, by staying and exploring it without a specific end in mind, but rather with an open-ended curiosity.

For a while when practising Chi Kung, I always came up against the same sensation. I felt slightly sick and like there was a painful ball in my belly. Every time this happened my thought train took me on the fast track to: I must have cancer in my stomach and all the scenarios that follow.

At some point I must have got fed up with this panicking run-away train, and I managed to jump off it. I reasoned with myself that I didn't appear to have any other cancer symptoms, the pain moved locations, and came and went only with Chi Kung and not at other times, and my general health was good.

I decided instead to investigate this sensation, and stop flinching and reacting every time it came up. I was able to feel through its shell, and if I really felt into its location it became smaller and much more pinpointed. I was able to explore it with my feeling senses and found that it felt less like a ball (or tumour) but more like a shifting red and black shadow, filled with bits of grit. This process of naming and describing the sensation bypassed my fear and my pathological imaginings, and kept me curious. One day it became blindingly obvious that the sensation actually wanted me to sit down, and stop trying to power and fight my way through. I didn't want to be the person who couldn't complete a form (my ego found that bruising), but when I listened to what my body was telling me, and sat down the sensation passed. By paying attention I knew when I could stand up and re-start the practise. I learned to feel for the first flicker of the sensation starting again (which I felt as a few pieces of red and black grit), I could react before it became difficult. I eventually, through patient practising, was able to sense the feeling and soften, give up the fight, and stay standing and continue with the form. The sensation taught me a lesson – a new and more productive, less confrontational way of practising Chi Kung.

Sensations may have different and varied messages, but I believe there's always a personal benefit in working with what comes up, even if it interrupts your practise. If we don't make the space to listen, we can't hear the message.

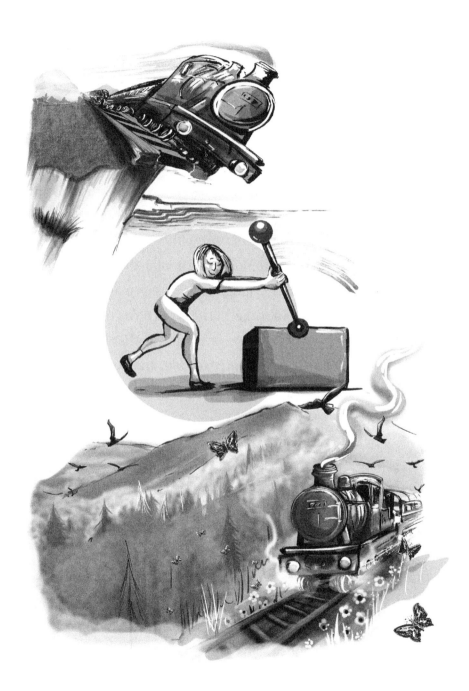

A note on Chi and the emotions

In Daoist philosophy and Chinese Medical Theory, the emotions are described as movements of Chi or energy. For instance; Worry is the knotting of the Chi, Anger is Chi rising upwards, Sadness is Chi sinking, Joy is expanding Chi, and apathy or depression is stagnating Chi. So, it follows that if we are able to manipulate our Chi, we will be able to affect our emotions. When we experience a particular thought / belief / emotion / situation when young, or in a big way, or over an extended period, our embodied emotions turn into energetic and eventually physical patterns or postures, that become our normal. By consciously practising exercises that impact our Chi (Chi Kung) we can begin to shift these ways of being, and feel into different ways of being.

It's not unusual in our culture, for emotions to be suppressed which in itself can stagnate Chi. For instance, suppose something very sad happened, and it felt like the sadness might overwhelm you, or perhaps sadness was not tolerated in your family and you learned not to express it, so you just put on a brave face and carry on. This would mean that Chi is not allowed to flow downwards, and might sit, sinking in the chest like a dammed stream, pooling. Sadness and grief affect the Lungs and Large

Intestines in Chinese medicine and so stagnant 'pooling' sadness could result in depression, or a tight or wheezing chest, or even problems with the lower gut. Each of the emotions also have mental and physical expressions.

If you are practising Chi Kung and any of this resonates with you, be gentle with yourself and remember Wu Wei – don't pitch yourself against how things are. Breathing and practising Chi Kung are really lovely, safe and forgiving ways to start to adjust and regulate the flow of Chi and soften any blockages.

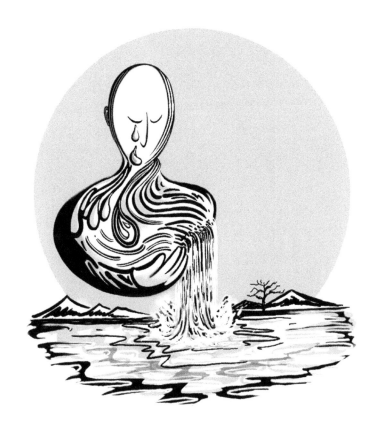

Chi Kung

Useful Acupressure points to know

I refer to these when teaching and describing Chi Kung exercises. It can be useful to get a felt sense of them by stimulating them. To do this and if you want to invoke the actions of these points, hold or press them with your thumbs or fingers for around 2 minutes, on each side. (A good tip is to press firmly but to imagine the tip of your thumb or finger is open and relaxed)

Bubbling Spring – Kidney 1. Just behind the ball of each foot in the centre line of the sole. This point is where we can imagine plugging into the ground.

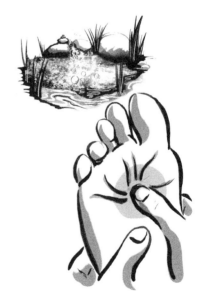

Lao Gong – Heart Protector 8. Translates as the 'Palace of Toil', but brings, coolness and calm to the emotions when they feel fractious. Almost in the centre of each palm – follow the web down your palm between the middle finger and index finger stopping level with the V of the web of the thumb and index finger (it will feel like the centre of your palm).

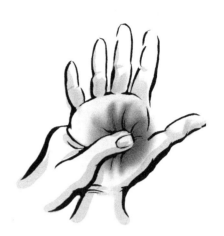

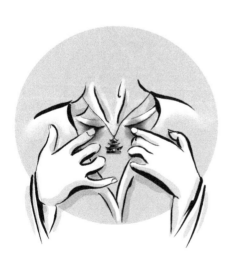

Mansion of approval - Kidney 27. Opens and relaxes the chest, and improves vitality. Emotionally freeing. A hollow just underneath your collar bone about 2 thumb widths out from the midline.

The Great Eliminator - Large Intestine 4. Generally good for pain in the body, and letting go both physically and emotionally. On the back of your hand in the web between the thumb and index finger. If you put your thumb alongside your index finger the crease will end in a slight 'hill'... where the flesh is slightly raised... that's the spot!

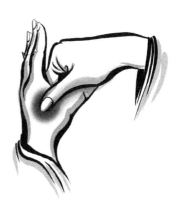

Heavens Pivot - Stomach 25. Great for any digestion disorders, as well as connecting the upper and lower parts of the body. This point is about three finger widths out either side from your belly button.

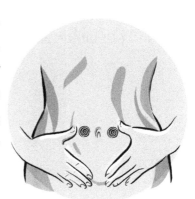

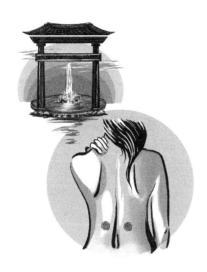

Ming Men, the sea of Vitality – We use Bladder 23 which is either side of the spine (Ming Men is actually on the midline, but Bladder 23 and Ming Men are intimately connected). This point is good for vitality in the whole body, and pretty much any pain or disorder! If you put your hands around your waist – fingers at the front and thumbs at the back – follow your thumbs around until you find your spine – then allow your thumbs to step up your back one step (about 2 vertebrae) and then a thumb width sized step outward from the spine. (so basically, a bit higher than your waist and just either side of the spine.)

Internal Energetic Structures

There are many meridians and extraordinary vessels and you can read about them at length in other texts.

The most important ones to understand and get a felt sense of in the context of this book, are your Dan Tien, and the bowl in your pelvis containing your Vital Essence or Jing.

Dan Tien

Your Dan Tien is your body's natural centre of balance, much easier to balance from than your head!

To find it most easily stand relaxed on both feet. Your Dan Tien is about 3 finger widths below your navel, and in the centre of your body between front and back. To initially try to get a feel for it, it can help to place your palm over that area at the front, and the flat of the back of your hand over the area opposite on your back which should be at the top of your sacrum or hips. Standing with your gaze ahead at eye level see if you can actually feel the centre of the space between your hands.

It's often described as being the 'pilot light' of your body. A bit like the flame on a boiler – if the boiler is working, whether active or not, the flame is there. It's similar with our bodies. If the Dan Ten is glowing, we're alive and our body is functioning. When we die that flame goes out.

If you really take your experience there (as opposed to your thoughts) you can start to explore your own Dan Tien; does it feel warm or cold, or liquid, solid or gas, does it have a colour or a texture? If you can't feel anything at all just imagine what it might feel like, even if it's just a tiny speck. Once your experience has landed there how does it feel?

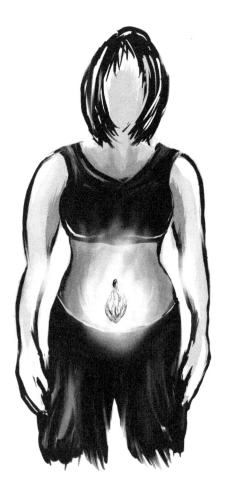

Bowl of Vital Essence

Within the physical structure of the pelvis is an energetic structure. The lake of vital essence, or Jing. Jing is the part of you that makes you the completely unique individual you are. Our aliveness is sourced from our Jing, the clue is in the name – *vital essence*. The quality and amount of your Jing is decided at the moment of conception, and lasts for your whole life. We can choose to spend it wisely or foolishly, to nourish and care for it, or to spend and spill it with careless living. When it is gone, it's gone. We stop being alive. Conserving and nourishing our Jing is therefore something well worth doing.

If you can imagine a skeleton, the bones of the pelvis almost form a bowl. There are bones at the bottom of the spine, the back of the pelvis, the sitting bones and the tail bone at the base, the pubic bones at the front and the hip bones at the front. There are no bones at the front of the belly however, and here we can help support ourselves and hold our bowl steady by having some strength or a sense of lifting upwards and inwards in the lowest part of our belly, to support the front of the bowl. The other place we can help ourselves is by making sure that the 'plug' is in the bowl – by having a lift (not a clench) in the pelvic floor. A combination of strength and relaxed suppleness in your posture mean that the bowl can be held safely, while allowing energy to circulate around and through the structure to nourish and energise.

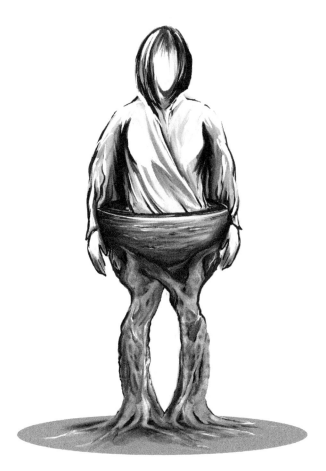

You can take your awareness to this bowl just as I described with the Dan Tien above. Explore it with your feeling senses, does it feel like a stone, glass, or wooden bowl, or one made of light or something else? Can you feel it standing on its two supporting pillars (your legs)? Can you feel the vital essence inside it, as a kind of syrup, or phosphorescent water, or a different liquid or gas?

The anatomical western description of this function, is that your belly holds your internal organs. Your life support systems in the abdomen are held in place by connective tissue or fascia, while being maintained and nourished by your transportation systems (blood and lymph). They are not supported by bony bowls, but by the lift, strength and suppleness in your fascia. The slight lift in your pelvic floor and strength in the lowest part of your belly helps to provide a gentle containment or holding 'floor' for all these essential organs.

An image I use to describe the energetic system of the bowl of vital essence and the Dan Tien, is that of an old oil lamp. The bowl of vital essence is the bowl of the lamp, full of lamp oil or Jing, and the wick leads upwards to the Dan Tien, the pilot light. The slight upwards pull of the oil travelling up with wick is the feeling of effortless lift in your pelvic floor and your lower belly.

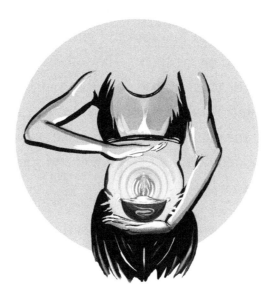

Wu Chi – Standing Posture

This is the basis of all Chi Kung postures and movements. If we're standing in Wu Chi, there is enough relaxation, softness and freedom for the Chi to flow easily through and around the body, and enough strength, space and structure for stability, holding us in an optimum position for the body to stack easily upwards from the ground or down from the heavens.

Wu Chi is referred to in the warm ups, so I've included the description of it here. However, for many people, finding Wu Chi will feel easier once the warm ups are completed.

Place your feet hip width apart, feet parallel as if they are on train tracks (they may feel as if they're turning in a little – you can look down and check). Imagine plugging your Bubbling Spring points on both feet into the ground or opening them as the ground opens *to* them. Allow the soles of your feet and the soles of your toes to feel the thin layer of contact with the ground. Your toes can relax on the ground without gripping, (assume there'll be no earthquakes and the earth can be trusted) and let the soles of your feet and soles of your toes soften to the ground.

Soften your ankles and knees (slight bend to the knees – try to avoid your knees folding in towards each other and keep them over your toes*). Feel that there is an easy flow of support up your legs and into your groin. Gently lift the pelvic floor** and have a slight pull to the lowest part of the belly, slightly tuck your tail enough to let the sacrum hang down towards to earth. Imagine the creases where your legs join your body at the front feeling open and soft.

Allow the spine to curve up gently through the centre of the body***. The shoulder girdle (made up of your collar bones and your shoulder blades) hangs off the spine, and the arms hang from the shoulder girdle. Have your arms hanging loosely and limply by your sides. Feel your rib cage hanging softly from your spine with space between each rib. Your head is balanced easily and artfully on top of your neck, as if you have carefully balanced a stone on its' perfect balance point. Eyes open and gaze softly into the distance at eye level****, your face resting gormless and soggy.

Your Dan Tien is balanced above your bubbling spring points (so your weight is not in your heels but further forwards), your Heart Centre is balanced above your Dan Tien and the centre of your relaxed head is balanced above your Heart Centre. Your balance and attention rests in your Dan Tien. You can imagine it as a flame, or a light, or a crystal – whatever comes to you.

*if your knees seem to want to fall inwards there are a couple of strategies to try. You can imagine that there is a ball between your knees holding them apart; You can slightly push your knees outwards creating some space inside your knees; You can imagine that although your feet are relaxed, you're being lifted up through your instep and up the inside front of your legs.

**This lift in the pelvic floor should be felt as a drawing up as opposed to a full-on clench. As I describe the bowl of vital essence and your Dan Tien being like an oil lamp where the oil travels up the wick from the well to the flame of the Dan Tien, there is an upwards movement but not an upwards pulling. If you imagine your sitting bones drawing together this could help you to find the sensation.

*** The spinous processes at the back of the spine are at the back of the body, but the body of the spine is further forwards, towards the middle of your body.

**** the eyes being open with a soft gaze is better than eyes closed. Although eyes closed may help you to use your other senses instead of sight, having a soft gaze is even more helpful. You can experiment with your gaze and find the effect for yourself, by focusing on a detail at eye level ahead of you and seeing how that feels, and then allowing your gaze to be soft and vacant, letting your peripheral vision to open, and see how that feels as a comparison.

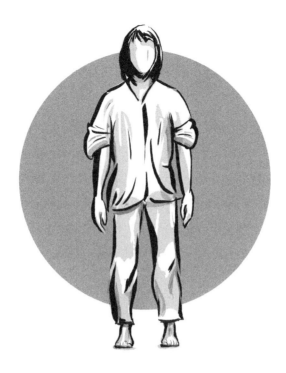

Standing in Wu Chi is itself a powerful practise. The more times you find your way into this posture the faster you will be able to re-discover it each time.

Standing still like a tree (as taught by Master Lam) begins with standing in Wu Chi for a period of time and is a wonderful practise – If you fancy trying it, maybe start with two to five minutes and increase only gradually. Standing Chi Kung is fully described at the end of the practises. Allow your attention to rest in your Dan Tien or scan your body, refining your posture by tiny observation and detail. Although it sounds simple standing still can be challenging. If a minute is long enough to start with then start there. You can slowly build up your practise, there is no hurry.

Why do a warm up?

The idea of a warm up is to get all the parts of your body awake, aware, moving, flowing and connected. Once our awareness has connected with the parts of the body, they're able to connect to each other, feeling like parts of a whole and not separate segments of a whole. It is often said that unless you do a warm up there is no point doing Chi Kung.

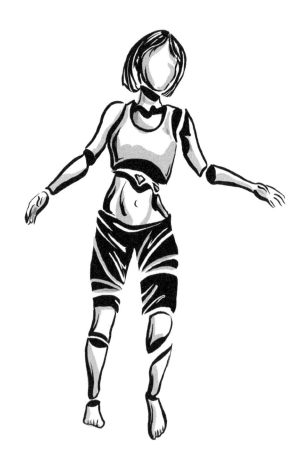

Practising without warming up means you are less likely to rebalance much, as you'll be working within your usual habitual and chronic (long term) patterns. If you're short of time, a warm up is a vital and complete practise in itself. It is just too easy to focus on the parts we like focusing on, and working through a systematic warm up gets all your body parts alive at once – even the bits you might usually forget about.

There are different versions of warm ups here. As with all these energy exercises, stay curious and enjoy finding out which one suits you in which situations. You can adjust the depth and speed of practise to suit the time you have available.

The Practises

Warm up one ~ The thorough one!

I've broken this down into 11 parts. With this warm up, once you're familiar with it, it can take five minutes or half an hour, depending on your focus, time available, stamina and what you hope to achieve. If you can, move easily from each body part to the next, moving off the spot when you need to, shaking your arms and legs out and then moving back into the practice. Taking half an hour over this warm up is a very complete practise in itself. I recommend that you read it through and visualise it for the first time before starting.

1) Warming up the head and neck

Begin by stacking your body upwards from the ground, with your feet hip width and relaxed soles of your feet and toes. Stand in Wu Chi. Be aware of your gaze softly focused, at eye level. Leaving the rest of your body as it is, allow your gaze to travel down the wall in front of you, allowing your head to follow, and slowly across the floor until you are gazing at your feet. Your shoulders haven't slumped, the rest of your posture is as it was, but your head is hanging on a soft neck. Take a deep breath in, and as you exhale allow your head to start to roll around to the side. Letting your head hang like a big heavy bowling ball, slowly and gently allow it to roll around through 360 degrees – so that the weight of your head gives your neck a lovely opening.

Slowly and gently are the keys here. Pause often to check that you are breathing, and not bracing, and release the neck and shoulders with the out breath. Allow the weight of the head to be relaxed without feeling like you have to protect your neck if you can. Try to stay in Wu Chi with the rest of your body. Go all the way round to centre in one direction then go back the other way. When you have been both ways, allow your gaze to travel back up to eye level, bringing your head softly with it. (NOTE.. If you experience pain or discomfort as your head rolls back, then use the alternative method 1B)

1B) Warming up the head and neck protecting the top of the spine.

Stand in Wu Chi standing posture. Taking a breath in and moving on the out breath, imagine that you are using your nose to draw a circle in the air. Move slowly and be curious about the range of movement you can feel. Circle slowly and small to start with and get bigger gradually as you explore. Remember to go easy side – don't push through any pain but relax or melt resistance. Take a breath in and move on the outbreath as you soften. Make sure that you try going both ways evenly. If you find a place that feels like it would like more attention, go back and forth over it compassionately, allowing the outbreath to melt the tension if it can. Allow your curiosity to explore your neck and jaw as you move.

Come back to centre and find the point of balance for your head and your eye level gaze.

If it feels good, move off the spot and have a shake-out before moving on.

2) Opening the throat and the front of your body

Stand in Wu Chi standing posture, eyes softly gazing at eye level. Allow your gaze to travel up the wall (or scenery if you're outside) and across the ceiling (or sky) above your head until you are looking upwards (as far as is comfortable). To avoid crunching at the base of your skull, feel that your face is being lifted skywards. Stay balanced in Wu Chi. Enjoy the feeling of opening from your jaw to your collar bones and into the front of your chest and torso. Purposefully allow your jaw to be relaxed – even if it hangs gormlessly open. Where the jaw joins the skull is the busiest joint in the body, with great muscle strength. Take this opportunity to really allow it to let go and to hang as you breathe here. Keeping your jaw soft, follow your gaze back down to eye level, without losing any of the height that you've gained. Your head pivots on top of your spine so that you are looking easily ahead again.

3) Opening the base of the skull and the upper back.

Stand in Wu Chi, standing posture. Again, allow your gaze to travel down the wall and across the floor until you are gazing at your toes. Your head is allowed to hang, really hang with all its' weight, although the rest of your posture remains as it was. If this is enough for you to enjoy a little stretch at the base of your skull, down your neck and upper back, take some quiet breaths here. Allow the weight of the head to hang 'unbraced' as much as you can without slumping the rest of your upper body. If you would like more of a stretch – link your hands and hang them over the back of your skull – elbows relaxed down and hanging and shoulders soft– as if your arms were a coat thrown over some bannisters. You don't need to pull your head down – the relaxed weight of your arms will be plenty. Take some quiet breaths as you soften on each outbreath. After a few breaths, allow your arms to drop by your sides, Whichever version you did, letting your soft gaze lead you, look along the floor in front of you and up until you return to gazing at eye level.

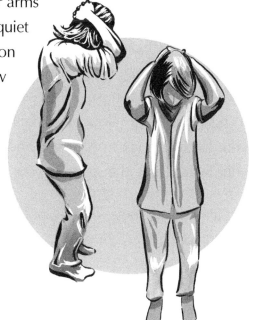

4) Opening the sides of the neck.

Stand in Wu Chi, standing posture. Keeping your gaze at eyelevel, and the rest of your posture facing forwards, allow your gaze to travel as far round to the left as you can, as if you're an owl. Take a deep breath and as you exhale release any bracing of your neck and shoulders – avoid forcing or fighting with your range of movement. Be aware of any tilting of the head – notice the difference if you keep your chin, nose and centre of the forehead in a vertical line. Come back to the centre and repeat to the right. Return to centre on an exhalation.

5) Releasing your skull.

Stand in Wu Chi, standing posture. Even if you don't know how to do the following, imagine that you do… Relax your jaw; your cheek bones; your nose; allow your ears to relax, stop straining to hear anything; allow your skull to relax and soften; allow your teeth to relax in your jaw and let your brain relax inside your head. Enjoy the space in your head for a breath.

If it feels good, move off the spot and have a shake-out before moving on.

6) Circling your arms.

Stand in Wu Chi, standing posture. With your arms still relaxed, and without using your shoulders at all (use magic instead!), allow one arm to start to move in a circle, as if by clockwork. Take your arm down, forwards, up and behind you in as close to a circle as you're comfortable with. Imagine your arm is the spoke of a wheel and your shoulder is the hub with your fingertips at the rim, the wheel is moving at a constant speed. Really enjoy and investigate the feeling of your arm and hand moving through space. (Don't worry if your circle is not round; let it be what it is and try not to fight your body.) Imagine your arm becoming hollow and spacious and light, and that it's lengthening all the way through the movement. It's completely effortless, as if someone else is moving your arm for you. Don't forget to breath at the same time! After about 6 circles, allow your arm to relax loose by your side, (you may want to pause here to feel the difference between your arms) and then repeat on the other side. It's interesting to note the differences between your arms.

7) Opening the sides of the body.

Standing with your feet hip width, reach your arms up and indulge in a lovely free form stretch, upwards and sideways, forwards and backwards. Planting your feet into the floor stretch out your armpits, the sides of your rib cage, the sides of your waist – as if you were trying to untuck any clothes that are tucked in. Make sure that you open your armpits somehow (there are some acupressure points there which will benefit). Walk or roll your shoulder blades away from the spine – and in towards the spine, your shoulder blades moving easily over your rib cage as if on ball bearings. Make more space between each rib, and allow the rib cage to feel flexible by moving it however feels good to you. Do any movements that help you feel open in your collar bones and breast bone. Come back to Wu Chi, standing posture and stand still to allow the changes to assimilate.

If it feels good, move off the spot and have a shake-out before moving on.

8) Lengthening the arms and opening the chest

Stand in Wu Chi, standing posture. Take your awareness to your Dan Tien… that means really feel into it rather than think about it. Feel that you're now balancing from your Dan Tien and not further up your body. From there, allow your hands to start to float out to the side away from you (not so high that your shoulders start to raise). Really let your shoulders drop and release on an out breath. Allow your hands to feel that they are floating away from you, lengthening your reach from the centre of your body. Keep allowing your hands to flow away from your centre on one exhalation, and allowing your shoulders to drop on the next exhalation. Check that you are still balancing over Bubbling Spring and if it's helpful let your knees bend rather than just be soft. After 6 breaths, slowly allow your arms to come back down, and allow them to hang by your sides. Take 3 breaths at least in Wu Chi while your body assimilates the improvement. You can follow this with 8-b, or just move on.

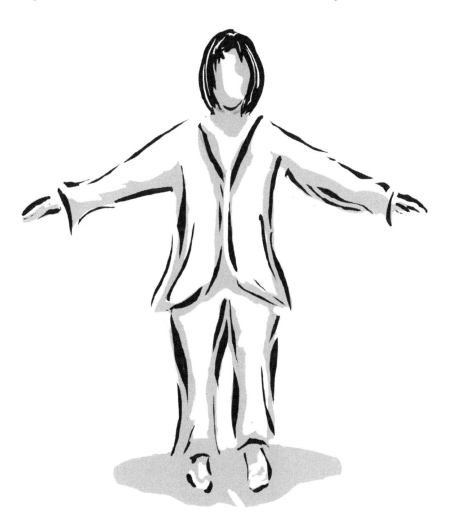

8-b) Opening the arms and Lung meridian and Lao Gung

Stand in Wu Chi, standing posture. Repeat the above exercise until the point where you are standing with your arms flowing out to the sides, shoulders soft. Staying in your Dan Tien and knees still soft, bubbling spring still plugged into the earth, (check that you're still balancing over bubbling spring) circle your wrists, first one way and then the other. Then open your palms and the inside (yin surface) of your arms to the sky, levering your thumbs back and open and rotating your whole arm from shoulders to fingertips. Your Lung meridian is now open and spacious, so take this opportunity to inhale and exhale deeply. Best time ever to enjoy breathing!

Then after 3 deep breaths, turn your palms away from you, as if pushing the walls apart, lift your fingers up towards the sky and your palms away from you, opening your palms wide and push through the heel of your hands, opening Lao Gung, letting go of anxiety and allowing calm to flow in for 3 more breaths (NB.. this may feel uncomfortable in your arms, if it is too much, soften them, bending slightly at the elbow if you need to and avoid bracing your shoulders to take the strain or fighting with your body in any way).

Keep your palms like that as you lower your hands as if you were going to place the palms of your hands on the floor. When your arms are down, allow the arms and hands to relax and hang. Breathe in Wu Chi for 6 breaths.

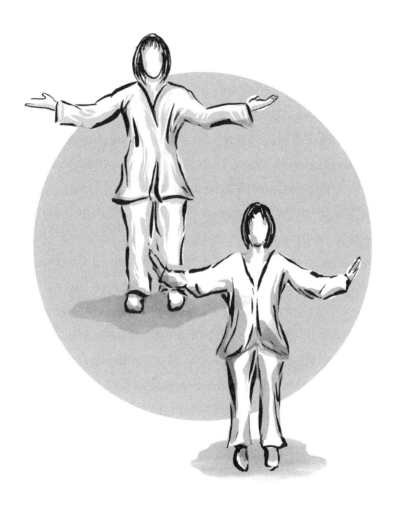

NB If you find this very tiring on your arms, don't worry! Be patient with yourself and take a break for a breath and then carry on if you need to. The strength will very soon build.

If it feels good, move off the spot and have a shake-out before moving on.

9) The bowl of vital essence in your pelvis

Stand in Wu Chi, standing posture. Take your awareness to the pelvis. Imagine a bowl sitting in your pelvis that contains your vital essence, your well of aliveness that is uniquely you, that you were born with. Gently lift your pelvic floor, effectively putting the plug in this bowl, and if you have the lowest part of your belly engaged, you'll have a front to this bowl. So, doing both of these things, imagine that your vital essence is the consistency of treacle, and staying in Wu Chi, circle the bowl (your hips) as if you were coating the inside of the bowl with your vital essence. This vital essence is precious but not fragile, so although we don't want to spill any, we also want to be relaxed about it. Don't forget to breathe. The circles can begin small and get bigger – make sure you go both ways. Notice how different parts of the circle feel, if you find resistance, allow it to soften rather than fight with it. You can imagine that this gentle moving is enlivening the vital essence. In the same way that the night sea can be phosphorescent and light up as boats or fish move through it, so your vital essence is being energised by this attention and movement.

You can expand your interest to include the physical structures and joints; the ball and socket joints on the outside of your hips, the joint between your spine and hips at your back, feel the sitting bones moving through space, your pubic bone, the hip bones at the front, your tail bone; mobilising, and nourishing as you move and breathe. When this feels complete move straight into 10.

10) Bowl of Vital essence opening further and lower back rest

Continuing the warm up of the bowl of Vital Essence, step your feet wider apart than hip width, and allowing the knees to bend for freedom of movement, continue to circle the pelvis and hips (keeping the pelvic floor and the lowest part of the front of the belly alive) and allow movement, softening and opening to continue. The Kwa (an energy gate at the front of the hips where the legs join the body) can often be tight and closed, so imagine opening a Lock gate in the area; freeing any stagnant water / chi to release, and allowing free flow of energy between the pelvis and the legs. When the whole area is feeling softer, bend your knees deeply and allow your whole body to relax and hang forwards and down. Allow the head and arms to hang. Have a rest here and breathe into your lower back.

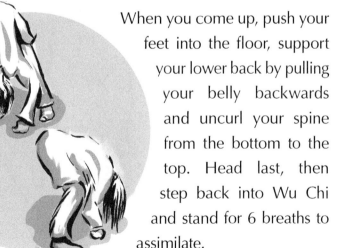

When you come up, push your feet into the floor, support your lower back by pulling your belly backwards and uncurl your spine from the bottom to the top. Head last, then step back into Wu Chi and stand for 6 breaths to assimilate.

If it feels good, move off the spot and have a shake-out before moving on.

11) Warming and moving Chi in the knees

Stand in Wu Chi, standing posture. Rub both palms together fast to create heat, and then with both hands rub one knee, over the knee cap, behind the knee, sides of the knees until all are warm. Then allowing your thumbs to find any holes in the landscape around, above and below your knees, and your finger tips to find spots behind your knees, steadily and slowly press and release to move on any stagnant Chi (keeping your hands as soft and unhurried as possible). There are some lovely acupressure points at the back of the knees so don't neglect this area. Continue this either for about a minute or until you stop enjoying it!

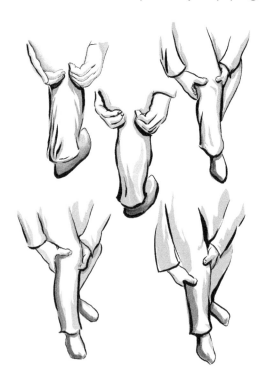

Squeeze and release your calves (don't squeeze and run your hands downwards while squeezing – this could be harmful for veins) and brush off your feet as if they were dusty. Repeat on the other side. Then stand in Wu Chi.

If it feels good, move off the spot and have a shake-out before moving on.

12) Moving the Chi at the ends of the meridians – warming up the toes!

Standing in Wu Chi, standing posture, make sure you are near a wall, chair or something you can hold for balance. With the heel of one foot, apply pressure to the top of the other foot close to your toes, standing on the web between each of your toes. Apply as much or as little pressure as you are comfortable with, moving your heel to work from the big toe towards the little toe across the top of the foot. Make sure that you're looking ahead if possible and still breathing and balancing in your Dan Tien. Then repeat on the other foot. Shake your feet as if you're trying to shake your toes off (one foot at a time unless you are exceptional!) come back in to Wu Chi, and stand for 6 relaxed breaths (breathing comfortably). Notice how your feet feel.

Stand in Wu Chi for around a minute. Allow the warm up to assimilate. See if you can feel your whole body as one flowing form.

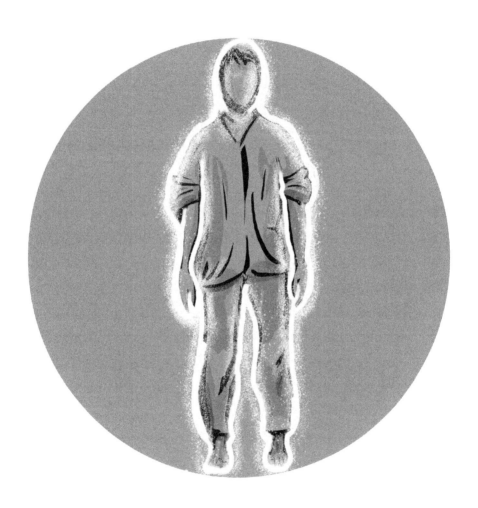

Alternative warm up. Do-In
(pronounced Dough-In)

This is a practise where we physically move the Chi by giving ourselves a percussive massage. NB You are both the giver and receiver of this practise so tailor it to what you enjoy – If anything feels uncomfortable then don't do it or do it less. As with all Chi Kung it is a conversation between you and your body – so don't forget to "listen" as well as "talk".

This is a really useful warm up to do if you feel you need protection, from a virus, from the weather, or even from a difficult relationship as it asserts your body's boundary.

Stand in Wu Chi, or can be done sitting if needed.

Head face and neck: Start by dropping relaxed fingertips from your wrists, over your scalp – tapping all around your head, including the base of the skull and around your ears, forehead, temples, cheek bones and jaw. It's a bit like a Chi shower and might sound a bit like raindrops from inside your head.

Between thumbs and forefingers pinch and release your eyebrows from the centre moving outwards – and do the same with your chin and moving out along your jaw from the centre.

Pull your earlobes and give them a stretch downwards, then pull your ears out the sides, giving them a stretch outward, and then up to the sky, giving yourself pointy ears! (otherwise known as the Buddha, Prince Charles, and Spok!)

Smooth your hands down your throat and sides of the neck. You can also grip and release the big muscles that run from behind the ears down the sides towards the front of the neck, one at a time.

Shoulders, arms and hands: Using a loose relaxed fist, tap or bang (whichever feels best) across the top of the opposite shoulder (on the soft bits, avoid bones!), and over the upper chest beneath the collar bone (including the hollow just inside the shoulder joint). If you want to include a sound here as you tap (entertains any young children nearby!) a long 'sir' sound will supplement the Lung Chi.

For the arms, tap / bang (remember loose fist) down the outside surface of the arm (upper arm, and the back of the forearm (an excellent place to stimulate your immune system)), wrists and hand, and back up the inside surface. Go down the outside and back up the inside of the arm three times, and a fourth time down the arm stopping at the hand and then swap hands and repeat on the other side.

With your thumb and forefinger pinch (front and back) the web between the little finger and the ring finger of your other hand. Pinch and massage for 10-30 seconds as far as you can reach into the web (you might be surprised how sore this is!) and then pull your grip away fast, away past your fingers, as if pulling stagnant Chi out of the web.

Repeat this between all the fingers. Between the forefinger and thumb where the web is bigger look for the most tender spot! Repeat on the other hand, then shake both hands as if you are shaking water off them.

Ribs, belly lower back and hips: Lifting your left arm straight up beside you (or as straight as is comfortable) with a cupped right hand or loose fist, tap / bang the left side of your rib cage working from under your arm / between your shoulder blade and your breast (or pecs) and work down following the curve of your ribs so that you finish on the bottom of your rib cage, then working back up. Repeat this a few times on each side. (optional extra – on both sides at once, tuck your fingers up and underneath your ribcage, starting about three finger widths out from the midline, and lean forwards over your fingers on an out breath. Move your hands one hands width further out and repeat. Only do this once.) Reaching behind you, as far up your back as you can comfortably reach, smooth your hands firmly downwards, over your mid and lower back, sacrum and bum, taking your hands off to start at the mid back again, and repeat 6 or more times.

Placing one hand over the other, imagining that you have something very delicate and yet powerful in your hands (you can use any imagery that works for you– light / a flame / a crystal etc) circle your belly with your hands (going up the right side, across the top and down the left side and across the bottom, but in a circular shape). You can work lightly or more deeply, whatever feels good. Circle your belly around 6 times.

Using loose fists, tap / bang your sacrum, your buttocks, around the ball and socket joint of your hips, the sides of your hips and the front of your hips. Do this for at least a minute with particular attention to the top of the buttocks and the soft part outwards of the sacrum.

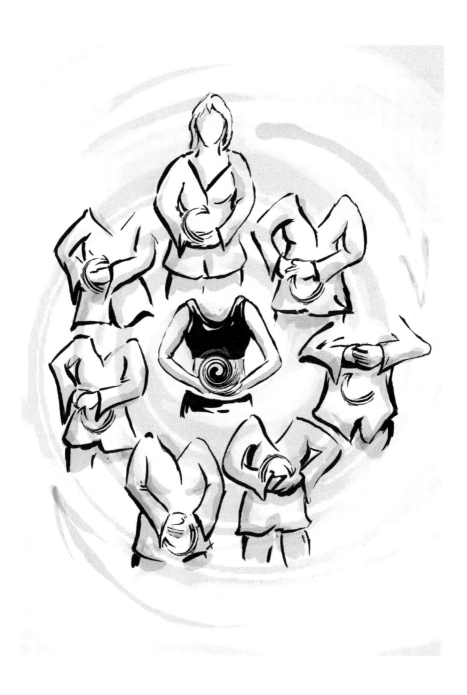

Legs and feet: With loose fists or cupped hands, tap or bang or clap down the outsides of both legs, and then up the insides – repeat 3 or 6 times. Rubbing your hands together to create heat take both hands to one knee and rub the knee – front and back, around the knee cap, sides of the knee and over the knee cap. Repeat on the other side. Then with loose fists or knuckles tap / bang down the outside of the shin, fairly firmly. Start at the top and work down 6 times each side, one leg at a time.

Taking hold of something stable for balance (if you need it) stand with your weight on the right foot. With the left heel use your standing weight to apply pressure to the top of the right foot near your toes, particularly working in the grooves on the top of the foot that run into the webs between your toes. Apply your weight and release, working from big toe to little toe. Then swap feet. Finish by shaking your feet as if you were shaking sand off them.

To finish: In any way that is comfortable using your palms, smooth down your body (as if you were smoothing the fur back down on a ruffled cat) from your head downwards. Smoothing your hair, face, neck and throat, over your shoulders and down your arms, chest, belly and back, over your bum and hips (especially the crease at the front of your hips) and down each leg and off your feet. Stand in Wu Chi or sit, for at least 6 deep breaths (or for 2 minutes if you can) to enjoy the sensation and allow your body to assimilate and make full adjustment to the flowing Chi.

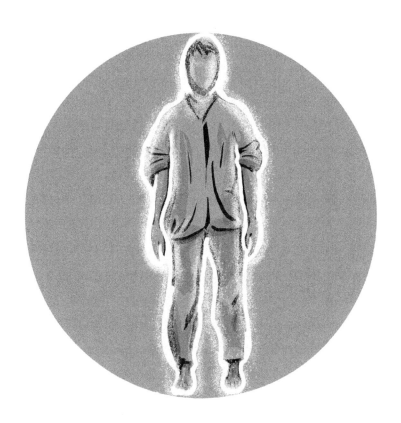

Warm ups you can do in secret!

These exercises are bitesize and can be done anywhere, any time! Probably easiest done in Wu Chi or in sitting posture, but I have managed successfully in school concerts and other covert opportunities. A purposeful exercise with active intention to create more space and ease, to allow Chi to Flow.

In these exercises there are not any obvious muscles you can work with – the invitation is to avoid feeling puzzled, but just imagine that you can do them. Although you can take your time with each one, they are accomplished almost at light speed – in a moment. Trying to sustain and force will cause contraction. Having said that take your time to allow yourself to really feel them, to allow the moment to keep renewing itself which is different from trying to sustain a sensation. Find the pace that feels easy to you, either singly or as a series of practises so just glide through them in your way. (When learning them for the first time the wonderful flow may elude you – panic not! We are all clunky when first learning new things!)

I.   Take your awareness to your skull, and relax your brain inside your skull.

II.   Relax your ears – stop straining to hear and allow sounds to either flow into them or not.

III.   Allow your cheek bones forehead and temples to soften and rest.

IV.   Feel / sense into the space between the root of your tongue and the back of your throat – empty space.

V.   Take a breath in, as slow and deep as you can without tensing or straining, and then with an open throat just release the breath out as fast as it naturally falls out… as you release the breath (anyone around you will just thing you are sighing!) allow your rib cage or let go of any tension.

VI.   Allow the protective layers of energy and tissue around your heart to relax and soften, front back and sides, the sensation a bit like swapping a tight pair of jeans for comfy PJs, freeing your heart from constriction and allowing the Chi around it to be supple and soft.

VII.   Let your kidneys, and the adrenal glands (on top of the kidneys) become more spacious and more supple. Enjoy the massage that your diaphragm gives them every time you breathe.

VIII. Do the same for the organs in your tummy, one at a time allow your gut and your liver, gall bladder, pancreas to relax and become more supple and spacious. (just imagine where they are)

IX.   Feel into your reproductive system and imagine it becoming lighter and more aerated – more like an Aero chocolate than a solid bar.

X.   Allow the soles of your feet and toes and the palms of your hands and pads of your fingers to soften and spread out.

XI.   Take a moment to feel your whole body as one harmoniously flowing form.

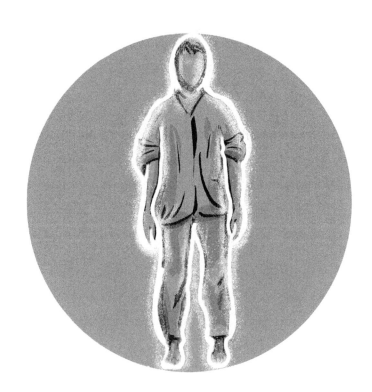

Sitting posture

Sit so that you can feel your sitting bones underneath you... if you're not sure, move around on your seat until you can feel them. Have your feet flat on the floor, if possible have them about hip width and parallel. If your knees want to fall in, just imagine a soft ball between your knees, or allow your knees to gently push outwards. Notice how this affects your feet, and double check that they can be relaxed on the ground at the same time. Your pelvic floor and the lowest part of your belly feel vibrant and lifted / gently pulled in. Your sacrum and spine resting down through your pelvis into your sitting bones – allow the tilt of your pelvis to find the best way for this to happen. Rest your hands in your lap, so that the shoulders are completely soft. If possible, gaze softly ahead (even if and when you close your eyes to practise, your gaze should be ahead through your closed eyelids) and allow the throat to feel open. Allow yourself to feel relaxed and open around Kidney 27, ShuFu (see acupressure points), so that your rib cage and shoulder blades can easily hang from the spine. If this changes the posture of your pelvis you may need to move your plumb-line slightly forwards, until you are balanced again on your sitting bones. Allow the crown of the head to float skywards (but don't push it!).

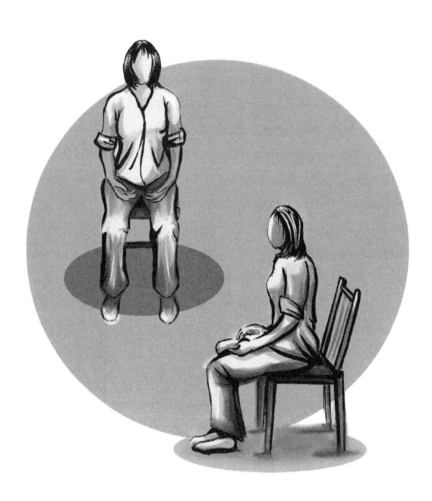

Short Practises to ground, open, calm, and direct your Chi / energy

Breathing into your body and out of your legs

Sit in sitting posture, either with a relaxed gaze ahead or you can close your eyes if you prefer. As you Breathe In, notice your upper body (torso head and arms), and as you Breathe Out notice your lower body (pelvis, hips, legs and feet). Purposefully Breathe In and Out to the same count, so that you are taking, even In and Out breaths, as long as is comfortable for you. Breathing In to notice your upper body, and Out to notice your lower body, for six or more relaxed breaths.

Let the focus go and watch your breathing return to normal. Bring your awareness back to the room.

Sitting with relaxed feet.
(good for grounding and calming)

Begin in sitting posture. Take a few comfortable breaths In and Out to the same count. Take your attention to the soles of your feet. Try to become aware of the thin layer of contact between the soles of your feet and the floor (or your socks or shoes). Notice how the pads of your toes rest on the floor, the heels, ball of each foot, instep (or how it rises off the floor) – the whole underneath of your feet. Return to the breath for 2 breaths.. Then start to imagine that your feet are spreading out and relaxing across the floor in whatever shape feels nice. For example, you might feel that you have enormous round feet, or feet shaped like flippers, or just one long toe. Stay with the sensation, following it as you breathe. Then bring your awareness to your sitting bones, and notice how they feel with the weight of the body resting through them. And then notice again where neutral is for your sacrum and pelvis, don't worry if it had crept back to its usual place – it's just interesting to note. Take your awareness back to the soles of your feet and enjoy any feeling of aliveness there. If you had no idea what feet looked like, and you had to go purely on the sensation of your still feet on the floor what would you guess that they look like?

When you feel ready, pay attention to your breathing, bringing your attention back to the room when you feel ready.

Listening practise

Sit or stand comfortably, this can be done either inside or outside, but have a window open if you're inside if possible.

Either stand in Wu Chi or sit in sitting posture. Gaze can be relaxed ahead or eyes gently closed. Take awareness to your breath and just observe how you are breathing for a few breaths. Then purposefully take three deep unhurried breaths (In and Out for the same count), and then allow your breathing to return to comfortable and easy. Notice your feet resting on the floor and notice your sitting bones on the chair, and your hands in your lap.

Notice any sounds you can hear, natural sounds, man-made sounds, sounds inside your body, your breath. Allow your attention to follow any and all sounds. Notice if you are straining with your ears to gather sounds, or if you're allowing the sound to flow into them. Try not to mentally list each sound and move on, but aim to keep allowing sounds to flow in whether they're the same of new. Practise this for a few minutes, or as long as is right for you. Don't worry if your attention wanders just bring it back when you can.

Now if you can, choose a sound that you can hear, that has a good feeling associated with it for you, and observe what you notice in your body as you listen to this sound. Does it affect your posture? Your mood? Your experience?

Relaxing your listening, take your attention to your Dan Tien, and stay for a few unhurried breaths with your centre. Allow your posture to reset if it needs to. Open your eyes to a soft eye level gaze when you are ready.

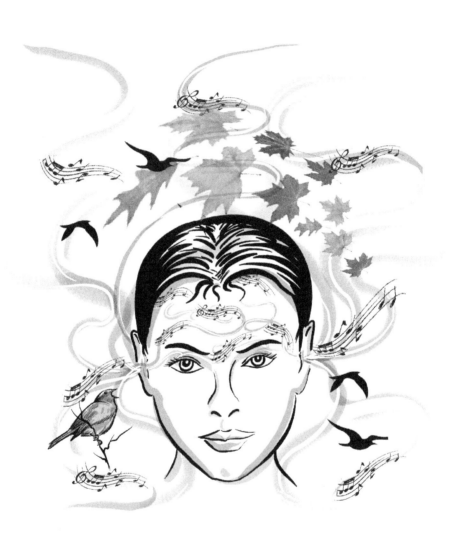

If I had never seen a hand...

This can be done as a sitting or standing practise. Stand in Wu Chi or sit in sitting posture. To do the long version you may prefer to sit. I have written this to take a tour of your Dan Tien, Hands and Feet, then back to the Dan Tien. It can easily be shortened to just the Dan Tien. Try to end with your Dan Tien so that you feel centred.

Take a moment to explore the sensation of your Dan Tien. Don't think about it but feel into it... explore it thoroughly, be interested in it, what shape, colour, texture or size does it feel? If you had to draw, paint or sculpt (or sew or... you get the idea!) your Dan Tien what would be the best representation of it?

When you've explored this, allow your focus to relax, and drift for a few breaths – breathing into the easiest part of your lungs.

Now take your curiosity and attention to your hands, either in your lap or by your sides. If you had never seen a hand, and were not allowed to look down, so that all you had to go on was the sensation of what you can feel at the end of your arms... if you didn't even call it a hand, what would your hands feel like? In the same way as you investigated your Dan Tien, how do your hands feel... how would you represent them, in feeling senses, or shape, temperature, colour, texture etc. Are they still or moving? Solid, liquid or gas? Consistent or transient?

Check back in with your posture and breathing for a moment. When you feel you have explored the sensation of your hands, allow your focus to relax and drift for a few breaths – breathing into the easiest part of your lungs.

Now take your curious attention to your feet, and repeat the same exercise, investigating with your senses, free of language, as if you had never seen a foot before. Exploring with curiosity what it feels like at the end of your legs. When you have explored your feet, return to your breathing again. Finally return to your Dan Tien. Feel into your Dan Tien as if you had not yet done it, it may have changed and you want to investigate this present moment. Then let your focus relax.

Take your awareness back to your whole body and your breath as you bring yourself back to your surroundings and end the practise.

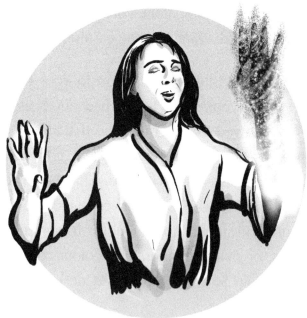

A route out of the shoulders

This can be done as a standing or a seated practise. Stand in Wu Chi, or sit in sitting posture with your hands comfortably in your lap. Begin by shaking your hands vigorously, as if trying to shake water off them, be enthusiastic and do this for between 10 and 20 seconds (Note – in order not to impede the flow from your shoulders, hold yourself stable as you shake your hands by being centred in your Dan Tien; alive in your pelvic floor and the lowest part of your belly). Pause with your hands resting in your lap or by your sides for a minute to allow the Chi to flow. Next with a loose fist of one hand beat the outside of the other fore-arm starting from just below the elbow and working down towards the wrist. Give the whole area a pummelling, to move stagnant chi and stimulate flow in the area. Turn your 'receiving' arm over and do the same on the inside of the fore-arm. You are both giver and receiver here so go as hard or as soft as you like! The looser your thumping fist the more pleasant this will feel. Repeat on the other arm, then shake both hands thoroughly again and sit or stand in good posture with your shoulders relaxed (but not pulled down) and your neck and jaw loose. Take 3 easy full breaths.

Now pay attention to your upper arms. With one hand make a loose fist and beat the outside (as far back as you can easily reach) of your upper arm, and across the front of the shoulder joint into the hollow of the chest and back along the inside of the upper arm. Repeat on the other side, then shake off the hands again and stand / sit in good posture (double check that your feet are relaxed on the floor, pelvic floor and lowest part of the belly strong – spine rising up easily through the body and loose relaxed jaw and skull).

With an In-Breath bring your shoulders as high up towards your ears as you can, really scrunching them up, and on the outbreath, release the air from your lungs on a sigh and allow your shoulders to drop. Pause for a moment and consciously intend them to stay relaxed at the level they dropped to. Repeat this so that you have done it three times. On the last time, after the out breath, make a decision not to stretch fidget or interfere with your shoulders. Just sit or stand with your balance and attention in your Dan Tien and watch and notice as the Chi finds its own balance and its own pathways.

Moving Chi Kung forms

I have described some of my favourite Chi Kung here, and also some of the simplest forms (they tend to be the same).

If you're starting from scratch without a teacher, I would suggest learning one form, and getting it comfortable and easy, before learning another. If you already have a practise there might be forms that are new to you, or reminders of familiar ones. It's unlikely that any two Chi Kung instructors teach the same exercise the same, so unless you come to my classes, you may enjoy new perspectives on familiar forms.

As a practise I recommend doing one warm up and one or two forms. If you have favourites it's lovely to stick to them, and likewise it can be fun to try something new. I like to finish with some standing (like a tree). I'm completely confident that if you are at all interested, you'll find your own way to practise, and my suggestions around timings, and length of practise are just suggestions. It is nice to have an instructor (or even a master for those who are lucky enough) but not necessary. It is also absolutely safe and good for you to follow where the impulse takes you. It's much more likely to fit in your life that way.

A note on all moving Chi Kung practises

Even if we have Wu Chi, standing posture really solid, as soon as we start to move it often takes us straight back to our old habits of how we tend to stand and move. Simple breathing is the perfect place to start to practise, to see if you are able to keep your posture balanced as you move. By keeping your posture in Wu Chi as you move you will get maximum effect from your Chi Kung. For instance, if your pelvis is tilted so that it tips forwards, and your pelvic floor and lowest part of your belly is loose, you will be losing vital essence, if your toes are gripping the ground and your knees locked there will be no flow in the legs and the Dan Tien will be tight and closed off. Learning to balance from your Dan Tien, nice and low down (like a Weeble) will be eternally useful.

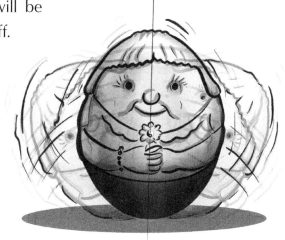

Another point to note is that there are no 'there and back' Chi Kung movements, there is no end point. The journey through the movements is just as important as getting to the end and changing direction. All movements should aim to be at a constant speed, and only arrive at the limits of the movement for a suspended moment, as the In-Breath turns to the Out-Breath and the Out-Breath to the In-Breath. Each and every part of the journey is important.

After each moving exercise

Chi Kung manipulates and builds our Chi or life force. During our lives we do all kinds of things to impede the flow of Chi, and even before that, we're born with tendencies and dispositions towards certain imbalances. These are compounded by our emotions, thoughts, physical patterns (and often injuries), life experiences that cause us to hold tension, reacting protectively, or bracing internally etc. If the Chi could flow unimpeded, the Yin and Yang would always find their own balance, the Chi always find its own way. Much of our Chi Kung is to both get out of the way and to encourage the flow of Yin and Yang. So – after each Chi Kung exercise stand in Wu Chi for as long as you feel the Chi still settling. Stand still and relaxed and balanced, and get out of the way, and let the slight change, the new normal settle in.

Chi Kung Forms

Rotating around your spine

Stand in Wu Chi, standing posture. Take some time to really align yourself – head balanced, heart stacked over Dan Tien, Dan Tien stacked over the Bowl of Vital Essence, Bowl supported over both legs and both legs balanced over the bubbling spring points.

Leaving both feet planted and both knees facing forwards, start to turn your head to look rhythmically from side to side, and allow your shoulders, spine and ribs to move with it, so that you are looking further and further round to your sides each time and then further until you're looking behind you. This form is a kind of swinging rotation from one side to the other side around a central pole (your spine), a freeing and loosening form that needs a certain speed to feel easy. Try to find a rhythm that feels effortless, twisting from left to right to left to right.... swinging from side to side. Your eyes tracking at eye level, moving from one point behind your left shoulder to a point behind your right shoulder etc. Let the turn to the right start the moment that the turn to the left finishes and vice versa. With your feeling senses be curious as to the location of your spine, as if you were pivoting around a slightly moveable central axis (which you are). You may notice that there is a section of your spine that moves more easily than the rest, or feels a little stiffer. The rest of your body can be just balanced and loose, which will look like your arms flinging round as you turn – a little like the strings with beads on that you find on a small hand drum that has a stick that you twist. Allow your In and Out breaths to find their own rhythm. You can enjoy the feeling of freedom in your ribs and arms, and the feeling of groundedness in your legs and feet.

Gradually let the movement become smaller, but still noticing your spine around which you're rotating, allowing your arms to stay floppy and eventually come to rest by your sides as you slow to a stop. When you come to a stop and stand in Wu Chi again notice what you can about your spine and the rest of your body. Spend a moment being curious and allowing any movement of Chi, or settling.

Emptying the shoulders

Stand in Wu Chi, standing posture. Leaving your arms completely relaxed and balancing from your Dan Tien.

On an In breath, leaving the shoulders alone to relax, allow your arms to rotate outwards so that the palms of your hands face upwards / out to the sides. The palms should be as open as possible, with the thumb pulling towards the back of your body, opening the palm. Without fighting your body try to have space in your armpits for an egg. This point should be reached at the fullness of the In-breath. As you exhale allow your arms to rotate inward allowing your palms to rotate facing backwards and then out to the sides, with your little fingers reaching out to the front of you. Try again to keep space in the armpits and have your palms open. You should reach this point at the emptiness of the Outbreath.

On the In breath rotating forwards, on the Out breath rotating backwards. Continue this movement with the breath, spiralling smoothly through the form and try to avoid going 'there and back' and holding each end point, instead allow the movement to take the same time as your breath does. Allow your breathing to dictate the speed, but there should only be a tiny moment of lightness between the In and Out breaths, between the inwards and outwards spiral.

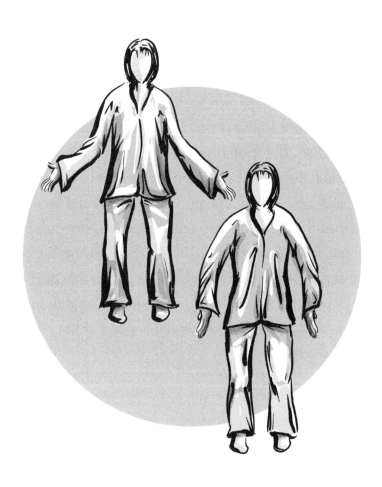

Enjoy the smooth unhurried soft rotation in your arms. Check in with your posture to ensure you stay balanced in your Dan Tien.

After you've performed this movement for between 1 and 5 minutes allow your arms and hands to pause in the thumb back position (the end of the in breath) for a few breaths, until you feel complete there, and then on an out breath allow your arms to rotate with the little finger forwards and again hold this position for a few breaths (ensure you are not fighting in your shoulders) until you feel complete, and then just release the effort and let your arms hang by your sides, as you get out of the way and allow your Chi to find its own balance and pathways. Take your attention to your posture, stand in Wu Chi until you are ready to move again.

Simple breathing

a) Basic

b) Opening

c) Breathing the legs to nourish and release

Basic

Stand in Wu Chi, standing posture – take the time to be fussy with your gaze, your Dan Tien and your feet. Relaxed but not collapsed.

Take a long breath in (for a comfortable count) and a long breath out (for the same count), with just a moment for weightless pause at the top and the bottom of the breath. Continue with the breath (adjusting it to feel comfortable if necessary), and allow the movement to follow when you feel ready.

The movement: In Breath - Hands come up in front of you – lifted by the back of the wrists, and arms raise to about chest height.

Out Breath – hands come down to return to sides. There should be space in each armpit enough for an egg (because why wouldn't you!) and your arms should be gently bent enough that they are softly slightly rounded (so not straight out in front of you but not close into your body either).

Allow your arms to feel that the expansion on the In-Breath is the thing that is lifting them, and the relaxation of the Out Breath is allowing them to sink back down. The inhalation is expansion, and the exhalation is contraction.

Make sure that you are practising at your own speed – making the breath unnaturally slow will create tension, at the same time allowing the breath to be a slow as it can comfortably be is helpful. (see note on breathing!). As you get comfortable with the movement, re-check your posture (commonly we might lean back as our arms raise up), and try to remain balanced from your Dan Tien, over your Bubbling Spring point, even though your arms are floating up and down, keep the lower part of your belly strong and alive and your pelvic floor slightly lifting.

Check that your shoulders have stayed out of the movement, and that your toes are not gripping the ground. Now as you continue the practise, feel into your Dan Tien, and notice how it expands and contracts with each breath.

Inhale – yang; expansion; gathering

Exhale – yin; contracting; releasing

Take a moment to notice that it's not only your breath, arms and Dan Tien that are following this pattern, but your whole body seems to expand and contract. All of your 30 trillion cells are expanding and contracting with your breath. Enjoy flowing with this natural rhythm.

Allow the movement to rest and wait in Wu Chi as you keep breathing, letting your arms hang easily by your sides, and stay in Wu Chi until you feel ready to move.

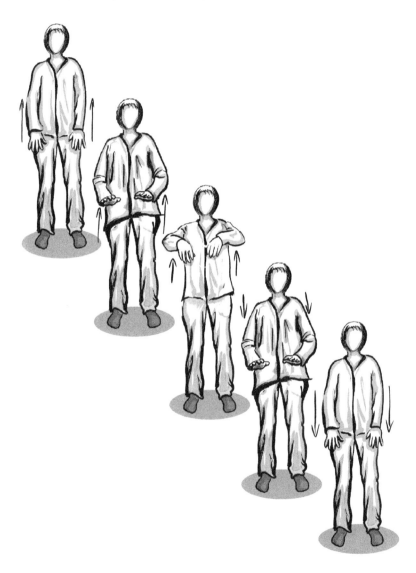

Opening

If you would like to create even more expanse, you can build on part one as follows:

In Breath: hands float up as before to about heart height, and then turn your palms towards you and allow your arms to uncurl (taking your hands out in an arc) until they are reaching out to the sides.

Out Breath: arms arc back towards your heart and then palms turn down as the arms come down again as in part one.

You will need to move slightly faster as your breath will stay the same length and there is more distance to cover. Once you have the hang of this allow your arms to start to become lighter, and let your shoulders relax, if your hands are coming up too high you won't be able to leave them alone, (don't pull them down on purpose, just allow them to soften). Check that you are still balancing from your Dan Tien over your Bubbling Spring points.

Notice the difference in sensation between this and the basic simple breathing. What different quality does the expansion and contraction have? Notice how it feels in your Dan Tien, and then how it feels in your whole body.

You could experiment with any of the following:

Spend 6 breaths, In and Out, really allowing the Out Breath to help you to let go of tension;

Spend 6 breaths, In and Out, feeling the expansion and contraction of your Dan Tien;

Spend 6 breaths, In and Out, feeling the circular nature of taking in and letting go of Chi.

To finish, allow your hands and arms to rest by your sides, stand in Wu Chi, as you continue to breathe in whatever way feels easy, and make whatever adjustments necessary to your posture. Stand until you feel ready to move, to allow your body to assimilate the changes.

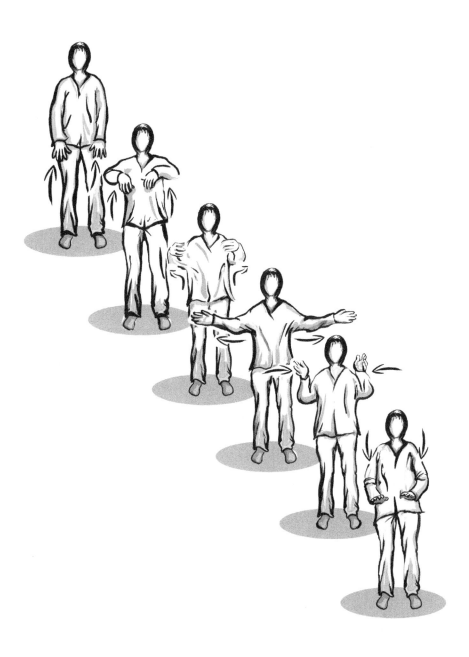

Breathing the legs to nourish and release

The form here looks the same as the basic simple breathing, so you will be doing the same movements. This is a change of focus / intention that fits beautifully with the rising In Breath and descending Out Breath.

Before starting, read the following brief explanation of the two meridians we will be working with.

Standing in Wu Chi with the knees bent over the toes for some people requires pushing the knees slightly outwards to avoid the knees bending in towards each other. The following Earth meridian can help to support and lift the inside of the legs.

It runs from the outside of the bed of the big toenail, along the instep of your foot and (if your leg were like a tall box) up the inside front corner of your calf, knee and thigh, through the Kwa (the join between the body and the legs) and into your

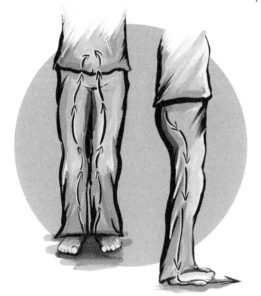

belly. This is one of the Earth Meridians.

The other is a meridian which runs from the middle of each buttock, down the outside of the legs, where a tracksuit stripe might be). It runs into the web between the 4th and 5th toes and into the outside of the 4th toe. This is one of the Wood meridians.

We'll think of the Earth as being nourishing and supportive – helping us to be easily upright by providing a lifting and holding energy, as if the earth is responding to our standing weight by bouncing back up our legs. The Wood we'll think of as the energy of flexibility (both in body and in life), allowing us to make agile decisions, and to change and bend like a sapling and not snap like dead wood, to flow smoothly.

For the practise, as we inhale and our arms lift (described in simple breathing part 1) we are drawing Chi up from the Earth, up the Earth meridian (front inside corner of the legs and into the belly) and as we exhale, we are softening and descending Chi through the Wood meridian (down over the hips and the outside of the legs).

Inhale – up the inside of the legs – supporting and nourishing

Exhale – down the outside of the legs – suppling and relaxing.

Continue with this breathing, staying balanced in your Dan Tien, allowing your easy unhurried breath to dictate the speed of your movement, moving all the way through, as Out Breath and In Breath give way to one another like waves.

After a few minutes, or as long as feels right for you, allow the breathing to continue but the moving to stop. Standing in Wu Chi allow your focus to return to your Dan Tien, as you allow the meridians to find their own balance. Be curious what you notice.

Breathing to take in, assimilate and release Chi

Stand in Wu Chi, standing posture. Have your awareness and balance in your Dan Tien. Turn your palms outwards (leaving your palms and fingers spread out but relaxed) and as you inhale bring your straight arms out to the sides and up in an arc, all the way up above your head (or as far as is possible). Turn your palms down as you exhale and bring your hands down close in front of you as if pushing a big ball down in front of your body, until your hands reach as far down as they will easily go. Then as you inhale turn your palms out again and repeat.

As you inhale feel the expansion of your lungs, your Dan Tien and your whole body.

As you exhale feel the Chi settling down through your body, as if you were smoothing downwards.

You can visualise pushing the Chi a little like you would push down the filter in a cafetière. Use your hands to guide the Chi down through your body – although your hands don't reach the floor allow your intention to follow the flow of Chi down to your feet and out into the ground.

As you inhale feel the Chi drawing up from the bubbling spring points in your feet, and in through your skin in your whole body, expansion in every one of your trillions of cells.

As you exhale feel the Chi settling into your body and releasing into the earth.

Repeat this movement following your breath, staying with the sensation and flow of renewal, and release. After at about 12 breaths or as long as you like, allow your arms to rest as you stand in Wu Chi and allow the Chi to find its own balance until you feel ready to move.

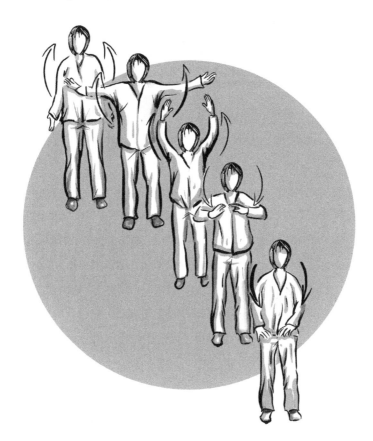

Horse Riding Stance

Traditionally called horse riding stance, but for those equestrians amongst you – more like a fat pony riding stance!

Step out so that your feet are about two shoulder widths apart in total (stepping half a shoulder width out on each side). Bend your knees so that you are 'sitting in your stance', so that you feel your centre of gravity – your Dan Tien - is low and balanced between your feet. Knees should be bent over your feet, try to avoid letting them fall in as it could cause problems, they might need to feel that they are pushing slightly outwards.

If you have problems with your knees make the stance as narrow as it needs to be so that you're comfortable, and ensure that you're lifting through the inside of the legs and that your knees are moving away from one another. Your pelvic floor and the lowest part of your belly should feel strong, your torso feeling as vertical as is comfortable and your head balanced easily on top of your spine. Your sacrum should be hanging down towards the floor, or even moving forwards, imagine your sitting bones moving in towards each other and your belly button moving backwards allowing the small of your back to open.

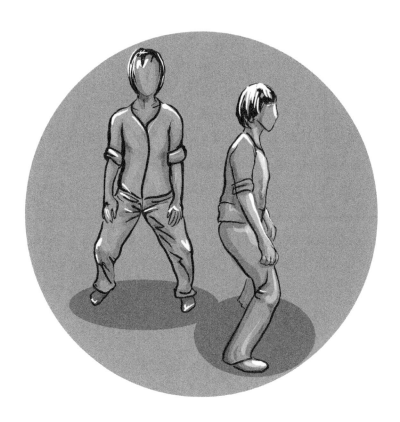

Waving hands like clouds

Stand in horse-riding stance. Take your right hand and hold it a comfortable distance in front of your left shoulder (about the length of your forearm), with your palm turned away, little finger skyward. Have space in your armpit for an egg, and your elbow and wrist softly bent. Have your left hand below your right hand (again about the distance of the length of your forearm) with the palm face up – as if supporting your right hand from a distance. Then draw both your hands across in-front of you to the right. Once past your body allow your hands to fluidly change positions, so that now your left hand is at shoulder height palm facing outwards and little finger to the sky, and your right hand is lower, palm to the sky, beneath your left hand. Now draw both hands across to the left, and allow them to again fluidly change. Repeat this as a continuous movement, trying not to speed up or slow down but feeling both hands floating through the movement with ease and softness, as if wafting your hands through clouds. Allow your gaze to be through the fingers of your upper hand and into the distance – letting your head follow the movement. There can be a little twist in the upper body as the hands move, but try to avoid twisting below your Dan Tien (hopefully your stance will stop you!).

Breathe wherever feels comfortable but do breathe, calmly and deeply. Remind yourself of the strength of the stance and re-set any parts of the horse-riding stance that you need to (for example legs strong and knees opening, hips open and weight balanced over bubbling spring). The strength of the lower body should enable to upper body to feel easy, light and effortless as your hands move like clouds.

When you have done this for anything over two minutes and/ or you want to stop, allow your arms to drop by your sides, and step back into Wu Chi. Wait until you feel ready to move.

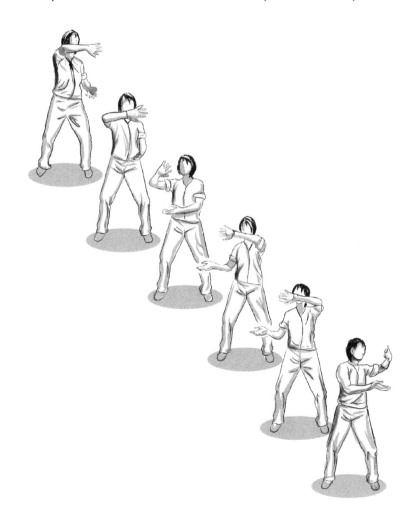

Scooping water from the stream

This sounds complicated on the first read, but once you have deciphered the instructions it flows easily. Have a couple of read through / walk throughs before you try!

Stand in horse-riding stance. Put both hands on your back – placing the 'great eliminator' on 'Ming Men' (see points!). Take a moment to feel your weight balanced on your bubbling spring, check that putting your hands on your back hasn't altered your posture (i.e you haven't allowed your back to hollow or crunched your shoulders to accommodate your hands). Imagine that you're standing astride a bubbling brook. Looking to your right, take your right hand off your back reach over to your right (at about 45 degrees from centre – so not right out to the side), lengthening your spine over to the right so that you're hinging from your waist. From there follow a kind of semi-circle movement as you scoop water from the pretend stream with your right hand, sweeping down to the middle and across to your left, coming back up. As you scoop, your spine stays long and your pelvic floor, belly and legs strong and stable. As you come up keep your knees really bent, but allow your torso to sit straight on top of your pelvis again.

Your right hand (which is now across in front of your left shoulder) turns palm outwards so that your little finger is skywards, still deep in your stance and space in your armpit for an egg. Draw your right hand across about a foot away from you in front of your face from left to right. Imagine that you are watching the water drip through your fingers, your torso stays upright, balanced in your pelvis, but you can follow with your gaze. Stay in your stance as your right arm continues on and moves behind you to plug back in - Great eliminator to Ming Men. At this moment your left hand 'unplugs' and you do the same movement on the left.. your left-hand scoops through the imaginary stream, as you come upright your knees stay bent, tail tucked, and then draw your left hand across from right to left, palm facing outwards as you gaze through the fingers at the imaginary water dripping down.

As you plug one hand in and release the other, Breathe In through the scooping part of the movement, and as you come up and draw your hand back across you Breathe Out.

Once you have a feeling of this movement the speed and flow should be governed by your speed of breath. Things to remember are: to keep your knees bent throughout, even when you come upright; when you come upright, bring your tail bone forwards and come back to horse riding stance; look for the lift in your pelvic floor and your belly to protect your lower back. This form is a lovely nourishing and strengthening practise, filling your reserves and regulating your energy throughout the day.

Once you have finished this practise with an even number of movements to each side, step back into Wu Chi with your hands still plugged into your back. Once balanced in Wu Chi you can let your arms relax by your sides and enjoy the sensation in your back, as your Gate of Vitality enjoys a Chi bath!

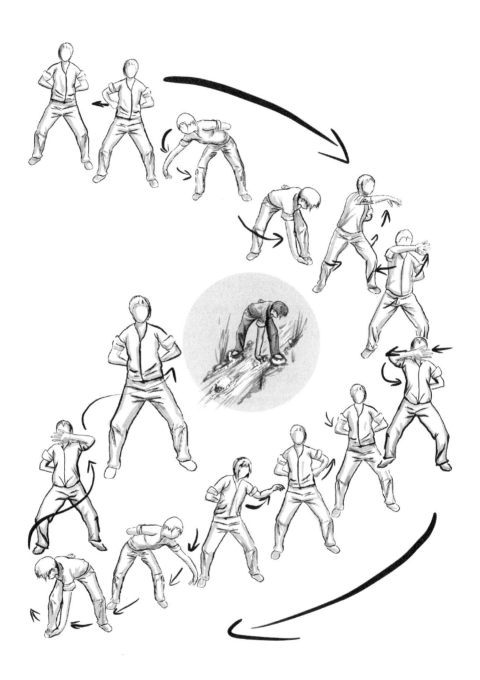

The Marriage Between Heaven and Earth ~ Hua Gong

This is a wonderful, powerful and complete practise in itself. It can be practised with many different focuses, and for any length of time.

I'll describe the movement and then describe the options of different focuses.

The movement:

Stand in Wu Chi, standing posture. Draw your hands up the centre line (hands dangling as if pulled up by your wrists) until they are at the level of your heart. Open and uncurl your arms, first opening the shoulder joint, then elbows, then wrists then hands and fingers, until you are standing with your arms stretching out to the sides, palms facing forwards.

Take your hands and your gaze upwards now, travelling in an arc up and out to your sides until your arms are reaching above your head to connect with the Heavens. From there, bring your hands down from above you, towards the top of your head, and then just off the body going down behind your head, flowing over the tops of your shoulders to the front of your body, and then heading down your sides, all the way down the sides of your legs and off the sides of your feet and toes to the floor.

As you go down your knees bend a little more, your spine curls forwards and the crown of your head hangs down as you relax down, bent and hanging. Having swept off your toes, your hands circle back into the centre line, fingers pointing down to the ground between your feet.

Draw your hands up the midline of your body, between your legs and upwards, by uncurling your spine from the base upwards (pulling your tummy towards your lower back) at the same time to come upright (at about the same time that your hands pass your belly). Keep your knees soft as you land back in Wu Chi.

You're back at the beginning, so continue drawing your hands up the midline until you reach chest height where you can begin to uncurl again. This is a circular movement and continues for as long as you like. When you decide to stop, your last journey up from the ground should stop at your Dan Tien, where you can hold your belly while you allow your Chi to find its own balance.

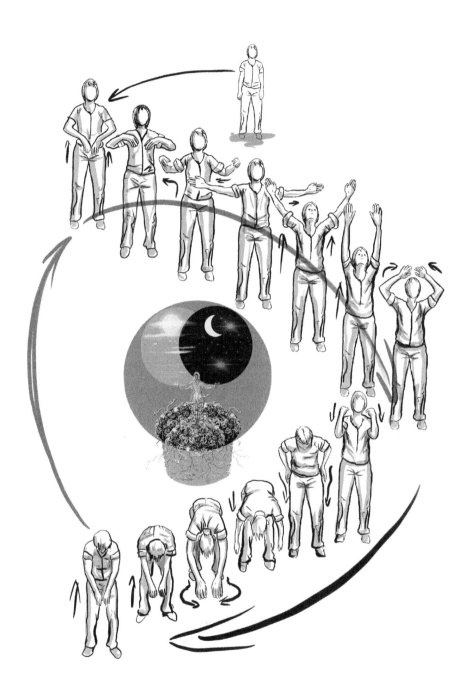

Intentions:

As you reach the point where your arms are stretched out to your sides you can think or imagine that you're connecting to people, your community, society in general, or just other life on the planet, connecting with the sociable part of ourselves.

As you reach the point where your arms are stretched above your head imagine that you are plugging your fingers into the heavens: blue sky, starlight energy, sun or moon... Heavenly Chi is Yang Chi – energising, warm, enlivening, light; and as you move you can pull this easily down over and through your body.

As you reach the point where your hands are down on or near the earth imagine that you are plugging into solid earth or a cosy earth den or cave, or the nourishing plants and vegetables that live in the earth; Yin Chi is nurturing, nourishing and containing, it is solidity and substance. Draw this sustenance up through your legs and torso to your heart. This focus can be your whole practice, or you can add to the intention a little.

Once you have practiced moving from connection with life, to connection with the heavens, to connection with the earth, you can take your awareness to your Dan Tien. See if you can feel those qualities reflecting in your belly... connecting with others, energising Yang Chi, and nourishing Yin Chi, how do they feel in your Dan Tien? Does your Dan Tien have a quality that is sociable, that is Energy, that is Substance?

You can also take your attention to the wonderful renewing flow of Chi that you are following, the enlivening flow of Yang Chi that flows constantly through your body, The support of the earth, the Yin Chi that rises constantly through your body, and the constant two way flow of energy between you and your environment / other people.

As you get comfortable with this movement you can take your attention now and then to your posture, checking that your feet are relaxed on the ground and that you are balanced over Bubbling Spring, that your belly and pelvic floor are strong, your knees stay soft and you are balancing from your Dan Tien and not your upper body.

When you feel you have practised this for long enough, let your hands rest on your belly, one over the other, and connect with your Dan Tien until you feel still and balanced. Release your hands, and stand in Wu Chi to allow your Chi to assimilate and balance. Notice how you feel, and stay in Wu Chi until you're ready to move.

More for the Shoulders

Stand in Wu Chi (or sit if necessary). Inhale, on the exhalation raise your arms out to the sides so they are reaching straight out from your shoulders.

Inhale and check that you're balancing from your Dan Tien. Exhale and bring your forearms up, to make a right angle with your upper arms. Make this as geometrically correct as you can, as if you're standing between two panes of glass and so cannot tilt or lean forwards or backwards with your arms and hands. If you're far from being able to hold this posture do your version, it just helps to have in mind the posture you're aiming at. On an Out Breath relax your jaw, chin and back of your skull.

On another exhalation turn your upper body as one unit, so that your hands arms and shoulders stay in the same relationship with each other as you turn – don't turn any further than you can keeping them aligned (so that your forward arm doesn't start to come inwards across your chest).

On the next inhalation come back to the centre. Wait there for a breath if you need to gather yourself and check in with your posture and then on an exhalation turn in the same way to the other side, and repeat for at least 3 times on each side.

To come back down from centre, straighten the elbow first, and then lower your hands until they are relaxed by your sides. Stay in Wu Chi for at least a minute to allow the stagnant Chi you have moved to really flow out of your shoulders.

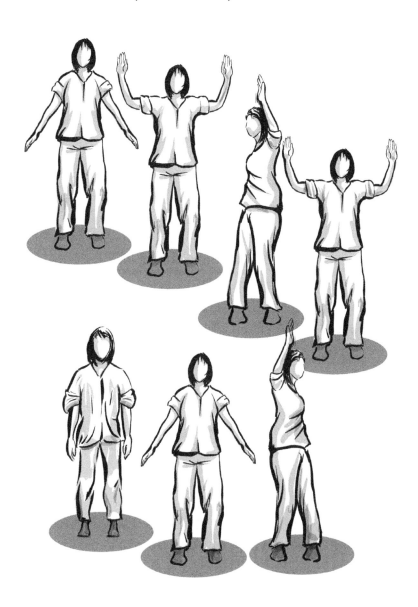

Playing with energy

Stand in Wu Chi, Standing posture. Imagine that you are holding a ball in front of your Dan Tien. With your gaze staying relaxed and into the distance allow your hands to slightly move in and out with your breath, as if finding and feeling the edges of the energy ball you're holding in-front of you.

Once you have a sense of the ball, staying well balanced in Wu Chi, you can start to play with the 'energy ball', expanding it with your In Breath and shrinking it with your Out Breath. You can experiment with enlarging it diagonally, vertically, any direction that feels right to you. If you try something and it feels not quite in your flow get curious and find where the flow might be. If you find a movement that really feels flowing, enjoy it for as long as it feels good.

Check in with your posture, and check in with where you're operating from. If you're balancing from and inhabiting your head, you may be trying to think this too much. Move to your Dan Tien, for both balance and awareness.

When you feel ready gradually allow the ball to become stiller and more stable in front of your Dan Tien again. Check through your posture and balance, and then slowly bring your hands in

to your belly, as if bringing the ball of energy into the bowl of
vital essence.

Rest with your hands over your Dan Tien for as long as you like,
and then for another few breaths with your hands by your sides
as you allow the Chi to assimilate and balance.

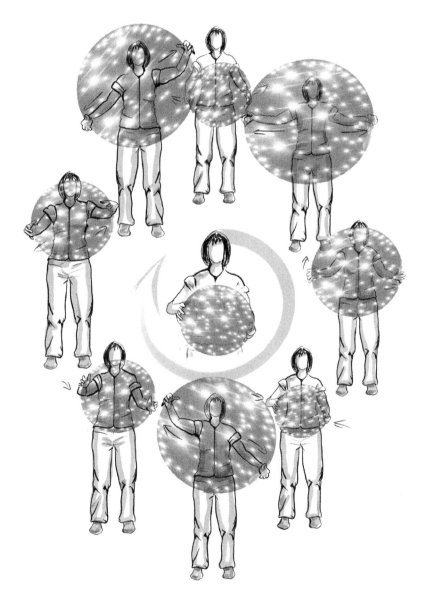

Circling a globe

Stand in horse riding stance. Hold an imaginary globe in front of your Dan Tien. You might like to imagine it luminous to help you to feel it.

Your gaze stays softly into the middle distance, and staying balanced from your Dan Tien over your bubbling spring bend your knees a little more and allow the globe to be held a little lower, between your legs.

Beginning by taking the globe to the left, allow your right hand to move in front of your left – as if turning the globe around in your hands, and then lifting it around in a large circle, to the left, up above your head and down to the right until you are holding the globe between your legs again. You can follow with your gaze. From there go back the other way, taking the globe to the right allow your left hand to move in front of your right and circle it out and up and over your head, and down to your left side until you are back where you started. Repeat this, continuing to circle first to one side and then the other.

The breathing: inhale as you do a semi-circle coming up to the top; exhale as you do a semi-circle coming down.

Your stance stays the same all the way through this exercise – keep a nice deep stance all the way through, even when your hands are above your head. Although you are moving your arms in the form, be aware not to work from your shoulders, but from your Dan Tien. It will be important to make sure that you have a slight lift and aliveness in your pelvic floor and lowest part of your belly. Be aware of the bowl in your pelvis as you circle, nourishing and enlivening your Vital Essence. Allow your head to be softly in line with your spine, or follow the globe with your eyes, but either way check that your face is soft, your jaw released and your feet and toes spreading across the floor.

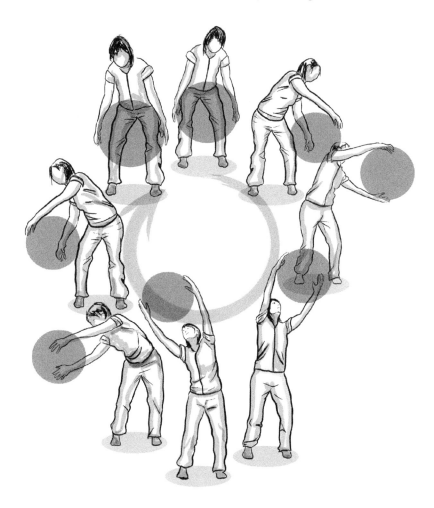

When you've done an equal number to each side, stop at the bottom of the movement and lift the globe back up to level with your belly. Slowly take your hands onto your Dan Tien, taking the globe of Chi into your belly. Step your feet into Wu Chi Standing posture, let your hands hang by your sides and stand for at least a minute.

Notice which parts of your body feel enlivened, the quality of those parts, and anything else that occurs to you as you allow the Chi to assimilate and balance.

Balancing the sides

Stand in Wu Chi, standing posture. Begin with your hands in front of your Dan Tien as if holding a beach ball in front of you. Your hands move in opposite directions at the same time.

Your right hand turning upwards and away from you as it moves up close in front of you to finish as if holding up the sky above your head with your palm face up and thumb forwards. At the same time your left hand turns downwards in front of you (and slightly to your side) and moves downwards to finish as if pushing down the earth.

Throughout, you stay in Wu Chi with soft knees and balanced in your Dan Tien.

On reaching the extension of the form, your hands both turn back towards each other and come back to holding the ball in front of your Dan Tien. Then you swap and the right hand moves to push down on the earth, and your left hand turns out and up and moves upwards to lift up the heavens.

The movement continues with the hands returning to centre and then moving away. Once you're comfortable with this form you may find that your hands skirt around the edges of the ball in front of your belly and don't need to return to a still holding posture.

To begin with the breathing is:

Inhale – hands separate

Exhale – hands return

Your awareness might be on the stillness of the centre point of your Dan Tien, and the two sides separating and coming together, or on the different sensations of the two sides. You may feel the opening and expansiveness followed by the release and contraction. You may also notice how different the two sides feel. Try not to make this a 'point to point' exercise but to move all the way through each movement with only the slightest pause or bounce back at either end and in the middle.

After some time breathing and moving in this way the exercise can be modified, with the return to centre being a little faster and more fluid, and rather than a pause for breath. It will be as follows:

Inhale – right hand moves upwards to hold up the heavens and left hand moves downwards to push down on the earth.

Exhale – right hand moves downwards, passes the ball in front of your Dan Tien and continues to push down on the earth. Left hand moves up past the ball in front of your Dan Tien and continues up to hold up the heavens. Continue in this way.

The focus here is on the sensation of Yin and Yang, and the flowing nature of Yin into Yang and Yang into Yin, and to remain aware of the still centre of the midline of your body and the Dan Tien. This will enable you to tune into your still centre more easily at any time.

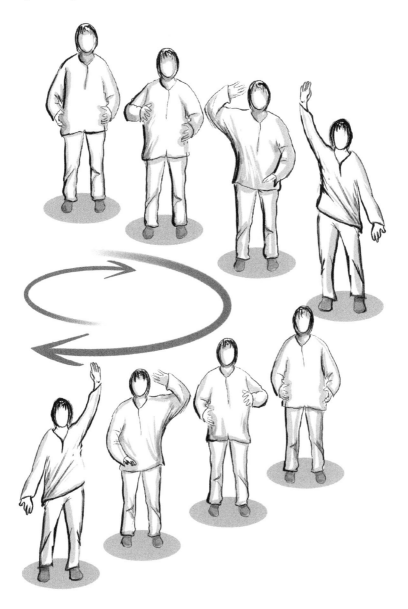

Our two sides will always feel different. During this Chi Kung you give each side equal space, attention and opportunity, and hold neither side as either good or bad, strong or weak; allowing freedom to flow without prejudice.

To end this practice, let your hands stop at the centre, and spend a breath holding a ball in front of your Dan Tien, bringing your hands slowly in to hold your belly, as if bringing the energy into your bowl of vital essence. Allow your hands to drop and stand in Wu Chi, and notice what you notice as your body balances.

Balancing to lift the diagonal

Stand a little wider than Wu Chi but not as wide as horse riding stance. Hands relaxed by your sides and gaze easily ahead into the middle distance.

To begin with, practise just shifting your weight - so that you are balanced over your left leg with the right leg empty, and then so that you are balanced over your right leg with your left leg empty. You can imagine shifting sands, filling one leg with all the weight – pouring sand into that leg, and then moving over the other leg and pouring all the sand into that leg. To start with don't lift either foot off the floor, but practise gliding from side to side. Try not to bob up and down, or tilt, but stay upright and at the same height throughout. Also don't be tempted to straighten your knees. It will help if you really make sure that you are balancing in your Dan Tien, you're just moving your bowl of vital essence over one leg and then over the other leg. Your gaze stays easily ahead, and once you have the hang of this it's as if you're gliding from side to side, from one leg to the other.

Once you're comfortable you can start to add in the diagonal lifting part! When your weight is over your right leg you just lift your left leg up so that it is either just hanging in space, or just dropping the toe onto the ground. If you lift from your centre, the rest of the leg can be hanging relaxed, or limply resting the toes on the ground. At the same time your right wrist lifts your right hand (leaving your shoulder soft, and no higher than brings your forearm at right angles to your upper arm) and dangles it as you balance on your right leg. Then, still balancing over a bent right leg, lower your left foot and your right hand so that your foot is resting on the ground and your whole arm just hanging, as you transfer your weight to the left leg and repeat on the other side. There will be a brief moment where you will be balanced in the centre between both legs as you move from side to side. The legs never completely straighten and the feet stay soft.

The breathing:

Inhale as you move to one side and lift the diagonal hand and foot.

Exhale to the centre.

Inhale as you move to the other side and lift the other diagonal

Exhale to centre.

Repeat this for a few minutes. If you are struggling to balance take some time to really feel into your belly and stay there as you move, keeping your balance actually in your centre.

Stand in Wu Chi for a minute or as long as feels right when you finish and have a moment to observe how and where your energy is after this Chi Kung. Even if you find it hard to do this form it's likely that it will leave you feeling centred.

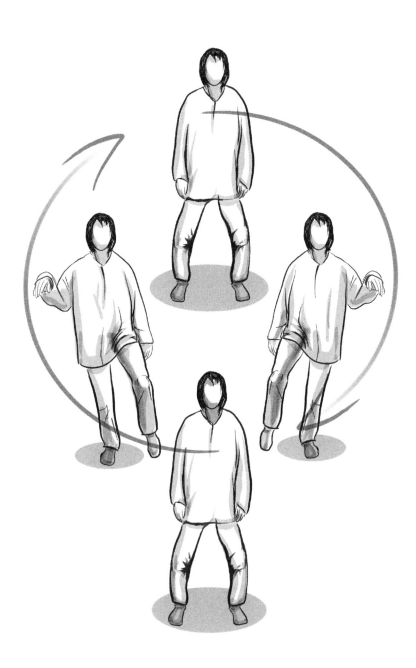

Walking Chi Kung –
Belly versus Head

There are many walking practises but this is something that is really useful in everyday life, and a fun game to experiment with.

You will need some space, so it's best to practise outside or in a large room if you can.

Walk for about a minute (either straight or in a circle or around the perimeter of a room) at a steady, 'normal' pace for you, and allow your mind to think -about anything; what you're doing later, what's for dinner, whether you slept well last night etc.

Stand still and notice how you feel.

Now, as a contrast, remember where your Dan Tien is, and energetically leave your brain and re-locate to your Dan Tien, and walk 'from' there. To help, you can imagine that your brain is now in your belly, or that you're steering with a laser that comes from below your belly button. Walk in this way, staying in your belly, at a pace that feels comfortable for about a minute.

Stand still and notice how you feel.

To compare and contrast, go back to your thinking way of walking, until you're back in your head, notice how you feel again, and then switch back to walking from your Dan Tien. Once you're confident that you're walking from your centre, enjoy it for as long as you want and then stand in Wu Chi and notice whatever you notice.

You can experiment with this at any time – walking your dog, on your way to an interview, round town or the supermarket… It gives you a very fast way to get out of your head and into your centre.

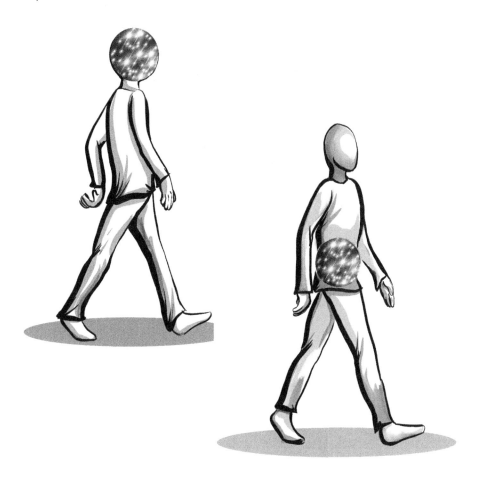

Digestive Chi Kung, combing through

Great to do after a large meal, with any digestive discomfort, or a lovely maintenance practise.

Stand in Wu Chi, standing posture. Before you begin, try standing with the palm of one hand over your belly and the back of the other hand on your back, opposite. Allow your centre of balance to drop into your belly. Then bring both hands to the front, one on top of the other, and circle the soft part of your belly in a clockwise direction with your hands. Move as slow or fast as feels nice. Keep circling for as long as you like.

Staying in Wu Chi take both your hands opposite your solar plexus, about a fore-arms length from your body, (just below your rib cage) at the midline, and let your hands curl slightly so that your fingers are pointing in towards you. Try not to compromise your softness. Imagine that you have lasers extending from each of your fingertips, that reach inside your belly. These lasers are going to comb downwards and out from centre to the sides through your belly. So, bring your hands (still off the body but with lasers pointing inwards) downwards and outwards from the centreline, with the fingertips still pointing in towards your belly. When you have combed through to the outside lower edges of your torso, allow your palms to turn upwards and bring your hands back up to start at your solar plexus again.

Exhale as you comb down and through,

Inhale as you bring your hands away and back up.

As these imaginary lasers comb through your abdomen they are smoothing, separating and soothing your Chi. Your abdomen contains your digestive, urinary, reproductive organs amongst other vital organs and systems. Imagine the whole of your belly being stroked and untangled (gently or firmly, whichever feels more pleasant) by these lasers as they penetrate softly through your body. They leave your abdomen feeling more like an Aero Chocolate bar than a solid slab.

After a few minutes or longer, allow your hands to relax by your sides and stand in Wu Chi. Notice how you feel.

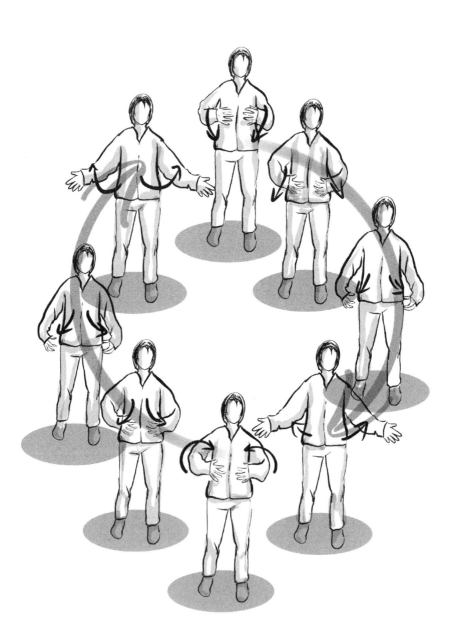

Deep standing

Deep standing is a static posture, that can feel like hard work but is incredibly beneficial. I was sceptical when first taught it (mostly as I didn't enjoy it, *at all*) but I have found it to really boost health in many ways, both for me and others, so I'm afraid it's well worth persisting with!

Take a wide stance, wider than horse riding stance if you can.

(NB If you have problems with your knees you will have to modify this posture to a point where you are comfortable, just keep brining your feet in until your knees are able to push outwards and be bent but are not in pain.)

Your feet don't have to be parallel if they don't want to be. Make a really deep bend in the knees, the fullest expression of the posture is the thighs parallel to the ground, but this is something to work towards for many of us. Have you knees actively pushing outwards, and pull your tail forwards underneath you, strong in the lower part of your belly as you pull your pelvis forwards and under you and your sitting bones in towards each other. Your lower back should feel quite open.

Balancing in your Dan Tien with strong legs, your upper body can now feel light. Let your arms float in front of you as if gently cradling a soft ball against your belly. Space in the armpits, your arms should feel like flexible light branches of a willow tree. Gaze softly ahead, face gormless and relaxed.

This posture is held for two minutes, or longer. If you find that too long it's absolutely ok to stand up, have a little rest, and go back into the posture again, but try keep doing that until the two minutes is up.

You will likely feel your thighs burning from the strain, which is okay. They may even shake, which is also okay.

One purpose of this form is to strengthen the standing apparatus of the body, to strengthen the trunk of the tree. We do so much sitting in our culture, and use our hands and arms to do things all the time. Sometimes we can resemble a plant with a small woody stem, weak roots, and big tough branches. It is no surprise that we get pain in our backs, shoulders and hips. Deep standing helps us to grow the tree trunk sturdy and strong.

You can even take the tree analogy a bit further and imagine (unless it freaks you out) that your legs are like strong roots beneath the earth, deep bubbling spring points bubbling energy upwards. Your Dan Tien is just above the ground and your light arms branch off the stem of your torso, as your head floats upwards.

When you have stood for two minutes (even if it's on and off) or longer (five minutes is something to aim for) as you build up your practise, stand up and use loose fists to beat your legs, on your thighs, backs of the legs, insides and outsides, all over your hips, and into your buttocks.

This beating keeps the Chi moving through and stops stagnation forming where there was static tension.

Once you feel appropriately beaten, stand in Wu Chi as you settle into balance. You might notice where and how your energy feels, it might feel like you a snow globe that's just been shaken up. Move when you feel ready, when everything has settled back down.

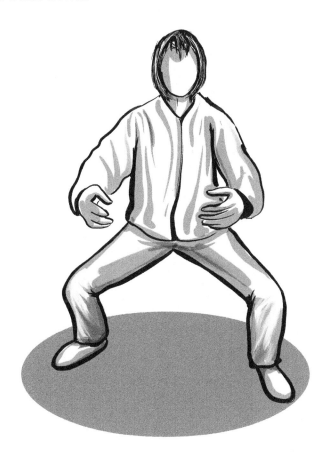

Standing like a tree

In this standing practise there are quite a few variations. I'll describe basic standing and a few further practise options. If standing isn't good for you this can also be done in sitting posture.

Stand in Wu Chi standing posture. Take some time to align yourself comfortably, checking that you're balanced in your Dan Tien over both bubbling spring points, bowl of vital essence supported and open, heart and head stacked above your Dan Tien, and the crown of your head moving towards the heavens. Initially you can stand with your arms by your sides.

Set a timer if you can or have a clock within easy view.

Notice how you're breathing; you can allow your breath to deepen but no forcing! You can start with anything from two to five minutes; go with what feels comfortable as a starting point. Your gaze stays ahead and softly into the middle distance.

For the time you've set, allow your awareness to either: roam your body, both physical and energetic, and offer yourself the opportunity to release and / or adjust your posture, but not by distracting yourself with big movements or scratching any itches; or, to settle in your Dan Tien and see if you can rest your attention there. This is where we get right out of the way and recognise the natural ability of your body to find its own balance.

As you progress you may want to increase the time you are standing (five minutes is a good place to aim for, or as you progress, ten or twenty minutes). Once you are relaxed and comfortable in this stance, you can if you'd like, progress to a posture with the arms.

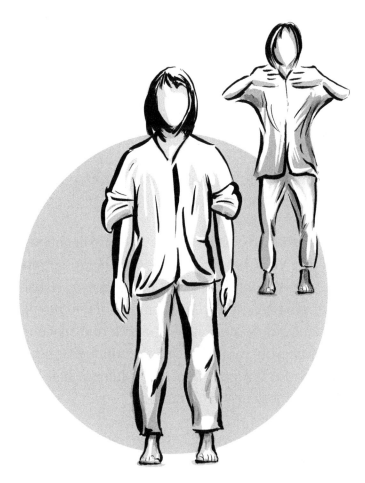

Additional postures for the full practise:

Standing as if holding a large ball in front of your belly.

Standing as if holding a large ball in front of your solar plexus.

Standing as if holding a large ball in front of your heart.

Standing holding your arms stretched out to the sides (palm forwards) a little lower than your shoulders.

Standing with your arms out to the side and slightly up with palms facing upwards, as if holding a large ball above your shoulders.

Begin your practise in Wu Chi with arms relaxed, it is a really beneficial posture and a practise in itself.

If you are doing all the postures in one practise begin by standing as described in Wu Chi for a couple of minutes, and then start at the top (above your head) and move down, holding each posture for between one and five minutes. If you are practising one posture at a time start at the bottom and make this your practise. When you can stand for five minutes and you feel confident, choose the next one up (holding a ball in front of your belly, etc) for your next practise.

You can't really do this wrong, as long as you pay attention to your posture while you stand, softening where you can and ensuring strength where you need it.

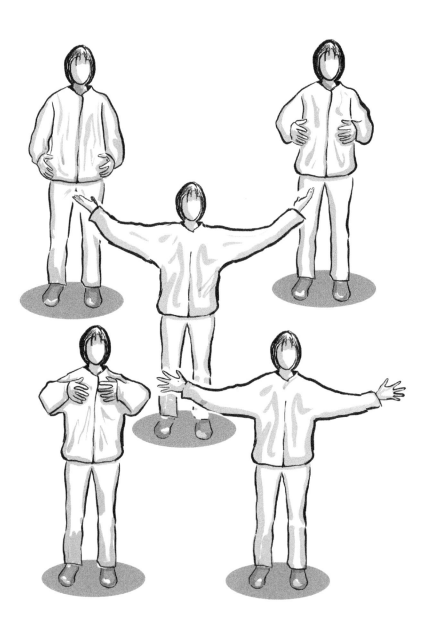

Living

Ultimately, unless we practice Chi Kung for many hours every day, we do more living than we do practice, and how we choose to live therefore has a great effect on how we are.

How we do anything tends to be how we do everything, and learning new ways of being through Chi Kung can spread through the whole of our lives, especially if supported by bringing consciousness awareness to how we live.

Taoist principles and my Chi Kung (and Shiatsu practice) have contributed greatly to shaping my life, my relationships with myself and others, and my philosophies. The teachings of Taoism explain things in such a way that once understood they seem to me to be fundamentally true, the kind of thing that's obvious but only once you know. So below, I've shared some of those principles, and extrapolated from them, hopefully making them relatable and relevant. I've quoted the Tao Te Jing in places to ground my points, as well as to illustrate and illuminate, sticking to my favourite edition which is the excellent translation by Stephen Mitchell.

Comparing and judgement

In many ways, in today's landscape, we can be easily cajoled into a competitive or at least comparative way of seeing ourselves and others. He's the best looking, she's way cleverer, I'm a slower learner, her life's so much more interesting... Social media may be accelerating this tendency, and not only for the younger generation, but it's pervasive anyway.

In the Tao Te Jing, Lao Tzu writes:

"When people see some things as beautiful other things become ugly. When people see some things as good other things become bad"

However liberal we may think we are, we all live both in judgement of ourselves and of others. These judgements can be anchored so deep within us that they're unconscious. Stripped back, these judgements are all comparisons. Either against others or against some unrealistic bench mark that we, our families or society have conjured up.

By calling being busy virtuous, the implication is that unless you're busy, you're lazy or lacking. Judge a symmetrical face as good and an uneven face as bad, and there will be few winners and many losers.

Every person is completely unique and therefore incomparable, and everyone has their own path to walk. When we hold up our accomplishments and our successes to be admired, we brush our failures under the carpet. There is no person or deed, who we should put on a pedestal, no one we should aspire to be like, no one we should compare ourselves to, and no standard that we should aspire to reach.

The Tao Te Jing tells us:

"True perfection seems imperfect yet it is perfectly itself.

True fullness seems empty yet it is fully present."

Our vital essence, our Jing, is our own essence, it's what makes us the individuals we are. If we can accept that in essence, we're perfect, then we can relax into ourselves and our outward expression will be more uniquely us.

Without comparison, I just look how I look, I just am how I am, and I am just having the experience of life that is unfolding before me.

This level of acceptance of ourselves and of others does absolutely not provide us with the ultimate get out or excuse to abandon personal responsibility. Nor does it mean that we're always right, or that we need not face our demons. Neither that we must accept judgement, disrespect or interference from others.

It simply means we can release the pressure of trying to be different from who we fundamentally are. In our perfection we're still imperfect, still human and fallible, still ever changing, growing and evolving.

There is the potential in every person to be an expression of their unique individuality, as opposed to an expression of expectations.

The Tao Te Ching tells us:

"When you are content simply to be yourself and don't compare or compete, everyone will respect you"

Writing this book triggered my own self judgement. The part of me that dreads comparison: What will my peers, students, teachers think of my work; how will my writing compare to others; is what I have to say unique or helpful compared to other teachers?

As a counter to this thought train, I come back to my base line; Am I writing what's authentic, or am I trying to be like someone else? I'm able to silence my 'inner comparer', as I know that writing this book as the truest expression of myself and what I teach as I can conjure.

If we want the freedom and the responsibility to live without apology or explanation, we must grant others the same respect. Comparing anyone else to our own measure is not only disrespectful but also can be unkind.

We can release our tendency not only to compare ourselves to others but also to not place our own expectations onto them. Our only responsibility lies with ourselves, being secure in the knowledge that no one is in essence, more or less worthwhile, whatever comparative measure you use.

Change and fear

Change and death are the only certainties in life. Everything else is somewhere on the scale of: predictable to the degree where it is almost certain; to, a complete shock, I never saw that coming!

The Tao Te Ching tells us:

"If you realise that all things change, there is nothing you will try to hold on to. If you aren't afraid of dying, there is nothing you can't achieve. Trying to control the future is like trying to take the master carpenters tools, chances are you will cut your hand."

As humans we like predictability, we love certainty and in general we fear change. Although predictability is always an illusion, as we never know what's coming, many of us still like to cling to the idea of it. We plan for and believe in imagined futures which may or may not manifest.

We sometimes source our security, our sense of safety, from our situation or from others or things, instead of from ourselves.

This challenges our ability to believe that we'll be ok.

Lao Tzu tells us:

"Whoever can see through all fear will always be safe."

The underlying fear, the only fundamental fear, is that we will not be ok. But what does that look like?

The ultimate 'not ok' must be death and dying. Accepting the inevitable yet unpredictable certainty of death would be liberating, if achievable. Instead, though, its unpredictability and it's ever-present possibility leads us to separate dying from living. In our sometimes-barren spiritual landscape, it's not often discussed, and rarely celebrated or prepared for.

When I was younger, I spent some time travelling in India. For a few weeks, I stayed in Varanasi on a houseboat on the river Ganges. This is a holy river and a holy place for many Hindus, a place where it's seen as fortuitous to die and be cremated.

During my stay there I became accustomed to the smell of cremation, and the sight of bodies in the river around me, as well as the sight grieving families. A very different experience to watching death and gore on TV. Death became both a very real part of life, and quite matter of fact, and the memory has always stayed with me.

I'm not saying that when death comes for me or those I love; I'll be all philosophical and relaxed about it. I fear suffering and loss, and doubt my ability to cope as much as the next person, (we've already established that I am a human practising Chi Kung and not a master teaching from an enlightened place).

Part of my ongoing practise of accepting impermanence, change and death has been solidified and embodied through my Chi Kung practise.

In every form, in every breath there is a taking in and a letting go. It can feel like a short version of the cycle of life. Each breath comes... and goes; each movement expands... and contracts; each practise starts... and finishes, and glimpses of bliss (if we're lucky) arise and then disappear.

This is, in a small way, practising change, and accepting that things come and things go. We find that the constant is our essence, ourself. As we become more familiar with our own Chi and our own sensations, we can source more of our security from within rather than without, from our knowing of ourselves.

Some of our fear of uncertainty leads us to try to manage and control our situation or people around us. We blame, governments, institutions, our partners and families etc. It's a kind of madness to think that the world and everyone in it should do what you want - in order for life to be acceptable to you. True contentment must come from allowing everything and everyone to be as they are, as you find your peace from within.

Fear lives in the future, and sadness in the past, but in the present moment, whatever your circumstances, you are ok. You may be in pain or discomfort, but you are fundamentally ok right now in this second. This level of spiritual mastery may be beyond many of us, but I have found it an invaluable working concept.

Even in the most difficult parts of my life, I've had a way to centre myself in my present. By practising Chi Kung. I've been able to accept that the whole universe is constantly changing around me, and even my experience of 'me' is in a constantly changing state around my Essence.

My Essence however is unchanging, beneath the layers of life experience and reaction that we all accumulate. The part that is completely unique to who I am.

The Yin and Yang of eating

Attitude counts

Before I start this subject, a quick disclaimer – I'm not a nutritionist, and I wouldn't presume to tell you what and how to eat. The range of dietary and nutritional advice available is incredibly confusing as much of it is contradictory. I do know that there is more to good health than eating right, and that eating right is an important ingredient of good health. I also know that eating right to one person will be vastly different to another.

In my pursuit of good health (which has driven much of my learning) I've found that the principles with which I practise Chi Kung are just as applicable to how and what I eat, as they are to how I move and breathe.

Eating well can be an emotionally charged subject, and as with all the practises in this book it's important to start from a place of compassion, patience and acceptance. We were never designed to live in a world where multimillion-pound industries are focusing their scientific and marketing might on persuading us to eat foods that we are simultaneously told are harmful to our health.

I'd like to suggest an empowered way to navigate choices regarding food. Cultivating curious interest, and non-judgement (which you have hopefully picked up by now in the rest of this book), works very well with investigating how your diet impacts how you feel. Trial and learning as opposed to trial and error.

We are all different and individual. It doesn't matter whether you've got a sensitive digestion and need a week in bed at the mention of dairy or gluten; or are someone who is robust and able to digest pretty much anything without missing a beat. It has no bearing on your worthiness or otherwise. We all have challenges, and opportunities to learn more about ourselves and they show up in all arenas of life. Your barometer to detect these opportunities is your body.

So much of what I've learnt from my Chi Kung practise has to do with the interest I pay to my sensations, to my Chi. Some has to do with trying something slightly different, or trying the same thing in a slightly different way, but it always comes back to 'how does that feel in me?'. This is easily transferable to how we approach our diets.

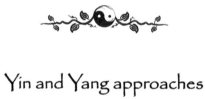

Yin and Yang approaches

There are vastly different diets eaten across the globe – The traditional Innuit diet has none of the varied fruits and vegetables that we are told we need, they stayed healthy on a diet of mainly wild animal fat and wild animal protein.

Conversely an Indigenous tribe in South America was found the have the healthiest arteries globally, on a diet high in plant carbohydrates and low in fat.

In searching for the 'right' one, it is important to put diet in both its internal and external landscape; of climate, culture, emotions, physical and other environmental influences. Oh the Yin and Yang of it all!

Don't despair as you don't have to wholly pick any entire approach. It's a case of trying things on for size and letting your growing awareness of your Chi, of how things feel, help you choose what works for you.

Digestion according to Traditional Chinese Medicine: Cold vs Warm

In TCM (Traditional Chinese Medicine), the model of how we digest has helped me step outside many detailed nutritional debates so I can see a bigger picture. It's not all about the right building blocks, but more about the ease of digestion.

TCM sees a nourishing diet as one that is undemanding on the digestive system, meaning that the body can easily extract what it needs from the food. Warm (or certainly not cold) and well-cooked foods are the easiest to digest and therefore the least draining on the body.

In Western nutrition, foods are valued for their contents, the constituent parts -so raw foods tend to have more undamaged nutrients, as opposed to cooked food where heat has destroyed some of the magic ingredients.

This means that a raw food diet is seen as beneficial to one school of thought, and damaging to another.

The digestion and assimilation of energy from food is described in TCM as follows:

Food descends into the Stomach which is depicted like a cauldron. Food's cooked in this cauldron (or as described in TCM texts, 'rotted and ripened) by the Yang energy of the Spleen, which is like a fire under the cauldron. Once properly cooked, it's ready to be assimilated into the body by the Small Intestine which sorts out which bits we need.

A meal that has come straight from the fridge to our stomach has to first be warmed through, until it's body temperature. If the food is raw, it will need to be 'cooked' for longer before it is ready to be assimilated into your body.

The longer the food needs to be 'cooked and warmed' for, the more drain there is on the energy of the Stomach and Spleen.

Depleted Spleen and Stomach Chi can lead to lumps, fat, weakness, sluggishness, a tangled or foggy mind, and sugar cravings.

With a largely cold raw diet, food is unlikely to be ready to be easily assimilated into your body, and there can be depletion, and undernourishment all round.

The difference in climate and environment (internal and external)

In Macrobiotic advice, we're encouraged to eat foods as they become available in your environment; In the UK that means salads in the summer, root veg in the winter, blackberries late summer etc.

Eating tropical foods regularly is ok if you are living somewhere hot and dry, but might be harder to assimilate in cold wet regions.

For many years after coming back from India I ate mangoes every day – I couldn't understand why anyone wouldn't as (in my opinion at the time) they tasted like heaven.

After being exposed to some of the macrobiotic principles, and at a time when my health was an issue, I tried a few weeks of substituting local ripe apples instead of mangoes in my diet.

Even from this one small change, I found I was less bloated, and less sluggish on rising.

Damp (as referred to under the heading above) will resolve given a warm dry climate, but you would never try and dry damp clothes on a washing line in the middle of a British winter.

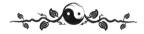

I spent a couple of winters living in a Tipi in Wales during my twenties. I was very physically strong and active, doing survivalish things like carrying water and chopping wood, and rarely suffered with health problems.

I had the same meal for nearly two years, from the same pot. I made a stew and kept adding to it. It bubbled away on the fire and was (incredibly) well cooked, and warm. Just what I needed as it was easy to digest and undemanding for my body.

This was a vital counterbalance to my living conditions, as Tipis were not designed for use in a cold and very damp climate!

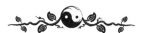

Another factor to consider is that the internal environment also includes your lifestyle, thoughts and emotions. Overthinking can knot the Stomach and Spleen Chi, which when weakened, can lead to sugar cravings. Ever found that during periods of intense study, even though all you've exercised is your thinking brain, you're craving sugar as if you have run a marathon? The internal and external environment can both effect and be affected by our food choices – and just to repeat – nutrition is only ever a part of the solution.

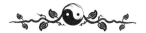

Undernourished vs detox

A detox sounds like a great idea, getting rid of the poisons and toxins in our body can't help but sound appealing, an internal spring cleaning! However, it's worth remembering that we're a part of our environment, and our water, our air and therefore most of what we eat, drink and breathe is doused in toxins, poisons and microplastics.

We can minimize a little by choosing organic foods and cosmetics where possible. It might sound depressing but it just is, and often, robust health can cope with these things.

The good news is that there is no negative or bad Chi that we have to detox from. Chi can become depleted, excessive or stuck, but there is none that is toxic. Indeed, excessive toxins can contribute to our Chi to becoming a little hot or stagnant, but we needn't take any bad Chi out as a remedy, just maybe clean up the causes of stagnation, or promote cooling. This a real relief, as we can free ourselves from the idea of having to purge the 'bad'. The answer is rarely just cutting things out of your diet.

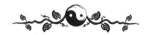

For many people the conversation around diet hinges on weight. People who are overweight as well as those who are underweight are often undernourished.

When we don't have the necessary Chi, or fuel in our body for it to work as we require it to, our body will start to crave more energy. We're more likely to become prey to the instant energy market of crisps, sweets, cakes, caffeine, sugary drinks etc. However, if we start to address this imbalance through depravation; by telling ourselves we must stop with the junk food, we haven't addressed the underlying issue of undernourishment. In this scenario we are almost certainly setting ourselves up for failure, as willpower may work for a while, but we will still be so depleted that we'll have no choice but to reach for instant energy again at some point.

A longer term and far easier and kinder strategy (based on the Taoist principles of compassion, simplicity and patience), is to recognise that we are depleted or undernourished. Our digestion will be weaker and so we could start to eat some foods that are both nourishing and easy to digest.

Soups or stews (bone broth traditionally is great at building Chi, but plant-based stews with pulses are great too) are easy to digest and full of easily assimilated nutrients. Rather than focus on cutting out the foods which don't nourish and by introducing more of the foods that do, as we replenish our Chi, the cravings will start to fall away.

Change your diet slowly if at all

By all means, try changing and tweaking how or what you eat. Or don't. If what you do now works well for you, why change it. If you do make changes, do it from a point of curiosity and interest, try to avoid hurrying and changing too much.

Lao Tzu tells us:

"The slow overcomes the fast.....In nature, nothing is hurried, yet all things are accomplished"

Even if you are in pain or discomfort and desperate for change, making dietary changes is only going to be one part of the puzzle. Maybe Chi Kung will be another part.

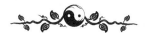

The Blame Game. Feeling stuck and what type of trying is useful

Where people live or work together, there will always be variation in the amount of effort we and others put in, in how we all behave, and how that makes us and others feel. We might think that if only people would do what we suggest, work harder, take more responsibility or be more efficient things would flow more smoothly, problems could be solved, or we might feel happier.

Lao Tzu tells us:

"Failure is an opportunity for blame. If you blame someone else, there is no end to the blame.

Therefore the Master fulfils her own obligations and corrects her own mistakes. She does what she needs to do and demands nothing of others."

We can all get stuck in the 'Drama Triangle'; either feeling like a Victim (poor me), a Rescuer (I can step in and fix this), or a Blamer (its his/her fault) (The Drama Triangle is a simple and yet powerful social model of interaction).

Although we're sociable creatures, our experience of life stems from ourselves, our own experiences. How much work, or lack of, do you put into yourself? Where could you be taking more personal responsibility, and where are you assuming the problems lie with others, or situations?

The Tao Te Ching teaches:

"Knowing others is intelligence; knowing yourself is true wisdom. Mastering others is strength; mastering yourself is true power."

It might then occur to us that we are both the source of our own problems and also the source of our own solutions, and have the capacity to make our own experience easier. This isn't intended as a stick with which to beat ourselves, but as an opportunity.

As I touched on earlier in this book, the balance between effort and letting go is pretty key, not only to finding balance, but to making any change.

Lao Tzu writes:

"Act without doing; work without effort. Think of the small as large and the few as many. Confront the difficult while it is still easy; accomplish the great task by a series of small acts."

Are you making effort in your life to address imbalance? Only you will be able to really answer this for yourself honestly, ignoring what you think you ought to do, what others do, or what others expect you to do.

As I've discussed previously, I'm not a fan of the thought that everything must be hard work. In fact, I have found that often instead of trying and trying and trying harder, the best course of action is often to take a step back and literally take a breather.

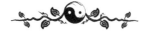

A few years ago, there was a part of my life that was refusing to budge. At some point I realised that although I thought I was continuing to try my hardest, I was a part of the problem, and not (as I told myself and anyone who would listen) just a victim of my circumstance. The 'trying my hardest' included all kinds of things such as trying to 'manifest' and going on dating apps, but not much serious internal excavation. Having been single, (interspersed with a couple of short-lived relationships), for a period of time, and not through choice, I realised that there was something within me, that was perpetuating the situation. It was not just that I was unlucky, I had a part to play in my own fortunes, even if I couldn't clearly see it.

(Please note at this point – this is absolutely not a game of blame yourself for everything that happens to you, but an offer to use everything that comes your way as an opportunity to learn more about yourself.)

I grasped the nettle, and took myself off to a therapist to explore my internal conditioning and patterns that could be an obstacle to being in a fulfilling relationship. (I can report that I am now no longer single and happily so!). There was no guarantee that in doing this I would get what I desired, but it was a way for me to find a route to flow around what felt to me like an obstacle in my life, and use it as an exploration.

When we find ourselves complaining about something, anything actually, we are allowing our Chi to bounce off the source of discomfort or blockage. Dropping our defences and paying gentle attention, instead of re-acting what has happened, and reacting *to* what has happened, can perhaps help us to expose and investigate, and eventually work around or dissolve the cause of the blockage. The type of effort required for this kind of truthful reflection can be a fairly seismic shift, and yet is wastes vastly less energy than staying stuck uncomfortably for years.

Justice and injustice: Conflict vs harmony

There are some things that are hard to just leave alone, and we feel we need to change them. It seems obvious to many that unless we fight for our environment and our planet, for economic / racial / gender equality, for justice / human / animal rights, then then nothing will change.

I agree that we've arrived at a time in history where we seem to be living at odds with many people's belief systems. Everyone has an opinion on how the government might do things better, or who is to blame and what for; the wealthy or the poor, men, or women, vegans or meat eaters etc.

Lao Tzu wrote:

"In harmony with the Tao, the sky is clear and spacious, the earth solid and full, all creatures flourish together, content with the way they are, endlessly repeating themselves, endlessly renewed.

When man interferes with the Tao, the sky becomes filthy, the earth becomes depleted, the equilibrium crumbles, creatures become extinct.

The Master views the parts with compassion, because he understands the whole. His constant practise is humility. He doesn't glitter like a jewel but lets himself be shaped by the Tao, as rugged and common as a stone."

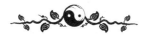

Lao Tzu showed amazing foresight having written this in the 4th century BC, as the relevance today is clear.

So how should we proceed?

I recently took one of my daughters to a large climate change protest. I agreed with the cause, and shared her concerns for the future of life on the planet and her sadness at the state of much of the natural world today.

I was expecting to enjoy the coming together of masses of people with a shared passion. It took me back to hear how much anger and hatred was being expressed. Many speakers seemed to be focusing on blame and not a shared passion or at solutions. We were encouraged to direct our anger at the wealthy, or at men, or at certain countries who had seemed to cause the problem.

If we take our lead from Lao Tzu we could start from a place of compassion, as opposed to anger and blame.

The remedy lies not in projecting our frustrations and disappointment onto others, but in being in harmony ourselves. My responsibility is to be compassionate to myself, and to others. I don't have the right answers any more than anyone else, but I do believe that the more I take responsibility within myself, the less I am likely to project on to others.

We all push the parts of ourselves that we don't like or that are socially unacceptable into the shadow of ourselves.

For instance, as a child you may learn that greed isn't acceptable. Perhaps a child instinctively felt some kind of a lack, and made any effort to fill it with whatever was at hand, but was told it was greedy and maybe disgusting. This could lead a person to grow up finding greed intolerable, to see greed as responsible for most of the problems in our world.

And yet those who are greedy are not evil, but simply trying to fill a sense that they don't have enough, that in order to feel safe or loved they need more. They could be an expression of what is in our own shadow.

Seen with compassion, all people are doing the best they can with the tools and knowledge they have available.

Our primary responsibility must be to untangle our own projections, our own shadows, to practise with our own bodies and sensations. While we are still feeling conflict in our body, we will still be adding the conflict in the world. If we can find more harmony in our body, we will be creating more harmony in the world.

Chi Kung is a way to practise not only accepting and finding flow within our bodies, but as we are only conversing with ourselves, it is an opportunity to be defenceless and curious about where we feel a sharp edge, or where we are bracing or fighting. By being more in flow as an individual, there will be one more flowing part of the human race, which eventually as a whole can start to return to a flow state.

Lao Tzu tells us:

"Return is the movement of the Tao. Yielding is the way of the Tao."

Taking action to create change is a wonderful thing to do. I'm not suggesting that we remain passive in the face of injustice, rather that in acting from our centre, we will be more likely to really listen and to be heard, more likely to create wholeness and less likely to create divisiveness. The Yang is allowed to become Yin and the Yin to become Yang; the polarisation is allowed to shift.

Lao Tzu writes:

"Nothing in the world is a soft and yielding as water. Yet for dissolving the hard and inflexible, nothing can surpass it."

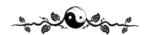

Micro-managing and Trust

I write this as a person with self-confessed controlling tendencies! Very recently someone pointed out to me that I wanted them to take responsibility for themselves, but only if they decided to do what I wanted them to do! Oops.

The Tao means 'The Way', and is the way of all things. When we are practising Chi Kung we're working on our own internal environment, and that includes our instinct to control and influence our surroundings.

Letting go of that influencing and control not only requires us to have trust in ourselves, (which we practice with Chi Kung) but also that everything and everyone else in the universe will find 'The Way' as well.

In fact, the more we try to control 'the rest of the universe' the more we are interrupting the flow of The Tao, and preventing things from finding 'the way'.

Lao Tzu teaches:

"If you want to be a great leader, you must learn to follow the Tao. Stop trying to control. Let go of fixed plans and concepts, and the world will govern itself.

The more prohibitions you have, the less virtuous people will be.

The more weapons you have, the less secure people will be.

The more subsidies you have the less self-reliant people will be.

Therefore the Master says:

I let go of the law, and people become honest.

I let go of economics and people become prosperous.

I let go of religion and people become serene.."

For the leader of a country to follow the teachings of Lao Tzu would take an enormous amount of trust, a leap of faith, and most people would counsel against his advice.

Instead, what is seen as more acceptable is to micromanage as much as possible, to allow people to have rights and liberties, but only within a tightly controlled framework.

I'm not suggesting that there should be no laws or regulation and that everyone would be lovely and there would be angels singing and utopia for ever. I'm just pointing out that many of us tend to do at a micro level, what the world is doing at a macro level.

I'm absolutely not making a political statement (many of us are triggered into divisive patterns by our differences in politics), but an observation of tendencies and patterns.

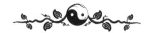

I was recently questioned 'Why should you think you understand ...(another's relationship trajectory)...with your tiny human mind?' She was right, why should we know what's best for anyone else? And why should my human mind be any better than someone else's, and better than trusting the Tao?

The Toaist wisdom on this subject makes so much sense to me – micro-managing is basically the same as taking someone's responsibility away from them, to ensure an outcome that we deem acceptable. The moment we frame another or others as passive, their lives become someone else's' responsibility and blame, victimhood, or rescuing follow.

Lao Tzu writes:

"if a country is governed with tolerance, the people are comfortable and honest.

If a country is governed with repression, the people are depressed and crafty........

Thus the Master is content to serve as an example and not impose her will.

She is pointed, but doesn't pierce. Straightforward, but supple.

Radiant, but easy on the eyes."

Whether we're part of a group of friends, parenting, teaching, managing co-workers, or even in local or national government, there is great value in practising tolerance and allowing others to make their own mistakes and learn from them.

Sometimes it can feel like we're managing something for good reason, for instance there are some mistakes a toddler should be allowed to learn from, and others that would be classed as neglect! When we're responsible for children it's clear we have a duty of care around their safety. Many parents (I include myself) find it hard to know where the line between managing for safety and managing for control lies.

However, with adults, it's even less clear. Sometimes we have to stop trying to fix / manage people, stop trying to save them from themselves, even if it's like watching a train crash in slow motion.

When we're protecting people from the consequences of their actions, we're preventing them from learning by experience. And that's only if we're right about our assumptions of where they are heading – sometimes the train never crashes and goes on to find new and unexplored territory.

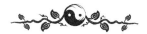

Finding the trust that everything will work out can be very tricky, especially when we live in a time where there is often much doom and gloom being constantly broadcast. I choose to only occasionally listen to the broadcasting. For me, the trust comes when I accept that the outcome may or may not be something I like or want. When I accept that my desire, although natural, is irrelevant, I'm able to trust, and to stay on my travelator as it scrolls through my life.

Lao Tzu writes:

"When there is no desire, all things are at peace"

Ending

I've used more than a few words to try to convey the essence of Chi Kung, the practise itself, and the application of its philosophies. Probably a few too many! My Chi Kung journey has been long and winding, taken many unexpected turns. Like the best journeys it has often felt fairly directionless.

Lao Tzu writes:

"A good traveller has no fixed plans and is not intent upon arriving. A good artist lets his intuition lead him wherever it wants. A good scientist has freed himself of concepts and keeps his mind open to what is"

I'll leave you to your own journey of discovery, and continue with mine.

"The Tao is like bellows: it is empty yet infinitely capable. The more you use it, the more it produces; the more you talk of it, the less you understand.

Hold on to the centre"

Bio

Lizzie Slowe grew up in North London, as a promising classical Cellist, and went on to briefly attend the Royal Northern College of Music in Manchester. After a few years of rebellion, she spent some time living in Brighton, London, living in a tipi in Wales and travelling in India. She trained in Shiatsu and Chi Kung with the European Shiatsu School under teachers including Chris Jarmey, Julie McBride and Daverick Legget, and went on to study at the Shiatsu College with teachers including Nicola Ley, Cliff Andrews and Pauline Sasaki. Lizzie worked full time as a Shiatsu Practitioner and teacher and Chi Kung instructor in London, Brighton and Ayrshire in Scotland, in settings including addiction services, substance misuse centres, refuges, health centres and private clinics, and teaching for the European Shiatsu School.

Before her two daughters reached school age, Lizzie and her family spent two years living on a catamaran, sailing in the Mediterranean and across the Atlantic Ocean to the Caribbean. She then moved to West Sussex where alongside her practice, she pursued her childhood love of horses, and now lives with her daughters, partner, horse and dog friends. Bringing her Taoist skill set and open-minded interest to owning horses, she qualified in Equine Shiatsu and Equine Facilitated Human

Development. She has co-founded a not for profit called 'In the Company of Horses' where she teaches and facilitates, and also privately practices Equine Facilitated Therapy and teaches Chi Kung locally.

Printed in Great Britain
by Amazon

79475644R00130